A King Washes Feet

A King Washes Feet

How to Love and Forgive Your Friends and Enemies— An Illustrated Bible Study

Jessica Claire Bond

a division of Baker Publishing Group
Minneapolis, Minnesota

© 2026 by Jessica Claire Bond

Published by Bethany House Publishers
Minneapolis, Minnesota
BethanyHouse.com

Bethany House Publishers is a division of
Baker Publishing Group, Grand Rapids, Michigan

Printed in the United States of America

All rights reserved. No part of this publication may be reproduced, stored in a retrieval system, or transmitted in any form or by any means—for example, electronic, photocopy, recording—without the prior written permission of the publisher. The only exception is brief quotations in printed reviews.

Library of Congress Cataloging-in-Publication Data
Names: Bond, Jessica Claire, author
Title: A king washes feet: how to love and forgive your friends and enemies—an illustrated Bible study / Jessica Bond.
Description: Minneapolis, Minnesota: Bethany House, a division of Baker Publishing Group, [2026] | Includes bibliographical references.
Identifiers: LCCN 2025016506 | ISBN 9780764245312 paperback
Subjects: LCSH: Forgiveness—Religious aspects—Christianity | Love—Religious aspects—Christianity | Bible—Study and teaching
Classification: LCC BV4647.F55 B663 2026 | DDC 234/.5—dc23/eng/20250611
LC record available at https://lccn.loc.gov/2025016506

Unless otherwise indicated, Scripture quotations are from the Revised Standard Version of the Bible: Catholic Edition, copyright © 1965, 1966 the Division of Christian Education of the National Council of the Churches of Christ in the United States of America. Used by permission. All rights reserved.

Scripture quotations labeled HCSB are from the Holman Christian Standard Bible®, copyright © 1999, 2000, 2002, 2003, 2009 by Holman Bible Publishers. Used by permission. Holman Christian Standard Bible®, Holman CSB®, and HCSB® are federally registered trademarks of Holman Bible Publishers.

Scripture quotations labeled NIV are from the Holy Bible, New International Version®, NIV®. Copyright © 1973, 1978, 1984, 2011 by Biblica, Inc.® Used by permission of Zondervan. All rights reserved worldwide. www.zondervan.com. The "NIV" and "New International Version" are trademarks registered in the United States Patent and Trademark Office by Biblica, Inc.®

Scripture quotations labeled NKJV are from the New King James Version®. Copyright © 1982 by Thomas Nelson. Used by permission. All rights reserved.

Scripture quotations labeled NRSVA are from the New Revised Standard Version Bible: Anglicised Edition, copyright © 1989, 1995 the Division of Christian Education of the National Council of the Churches of Christ in the United States of America. Used by permission. All rights reserved.

This book has been theologically reviewed by Fr. Ken Barker MGL.

Cover art illustrated by Jessica Claire Bond
Cover design by Chris Kuhatschek
Interior illustrations by Jessica Claire Bond
Author photo © Efraim Tam

The Author is represented by Alive Literary Agency, www.aliveliterary.com.

Baker Publishing Group publications use paper produced from sustainable forestry practices and postconsumer waste whenever possible.

26 27 28 29 30 31 32   7 6 5 4 3 2 1

Contents

Foreword by Kris Vallotton   9
Foreword by Father Rob Galea   11
Introduction   13

Jesus

1. A King in a Crowd   21
2. The Servant King   25
3. More Radical Than We Think   29
4. Too Much and Not Enough   33
5. Unworthy   37
6. Barabbas Is Me   41
7. We Killed God   47
8. Scars   51
9. The Charcoal Fire   55

You

10. Washing the Bride   61
11. Anointing the Bridegroom   67
12. If You Can't Grab His Hands   71
13. Interrupting Good Plans   78
14. Healing Trauma   81
15. Your Worship Is Never a Waste   89

16. Keeping Your Heart Soft   95
17. Love Is a Decision   99
18. True Love and Free Will   106
19. Performance   109
20. Repetitive Failure   115

Friends

21. Love Looks Like Something   121
22. The Temperature of the Water   125
23. Separating Identity from Behavior   129
24. Go Where the People Are   135
25. Reach for the Towel, Not Rocks   139
26. Wash and Be Washed   143
27. Forgiving Your Parents   149
28. Run Toward Prodigals   155
29. Feeding Celebrities to Lions   159
30. Protecting People   163
31. The People Missing from Our Pews   167
32. Canceling Cancel Culture   173

Enemies

33. He Washed Judas's Feet Too   179
34. Honoring Our Enemies   183
35. Politics   187
36. A Heart for Both Sides   194
37. Prostitutes at the Dining Table   199
38. Today's Tax Collectors   205
39. When They Don't Say Sorry   209
40. Who You Need to See on the Seat   215

Acknowledgements   220
Notes   222

For my Jesus, who washed my feet first, and for my mother, who has washed them a thousand times since.

Trigger Warning

This book is about real life. We need footwashing because we need Jesus to burst into the parts of our stories that hurt the most, and to wash us after the places we've walked.

This book mentions subjects such as domestic violence, adultery, sexual abuse, suicide, pornography, trauma, earthquakes, death, abortion, religious persecution, and human trafficking. If these are sensitive topics for you, please be aware. But I pray that the Jesus you meet through these pages—and the way these topics are approached—brings healing. Perhaps this book was written exactly for you.

Foreword

We live in a world obsessed with chasing titles, power, and followers like they'll save us. But the true King, the One who spoke galaxies into being, didn't come with a scepter in His hand. He came with a towel. And He didn't sit on a throne, He knelt low.

Jessica Bond has written something more than a book. She's handed us a mirror. Her words are soaked in Scripture, dripping with revelation, and grounded in gritty, gut-level honesty.

As you turn the pages of this book, you will be reminded that the gospel isn't a story of a God who kept His distance from our messes. No, our God got on His knees, wrapped himself in a towel, and scrubbed the dirt from the very feet that would run away, deny Him, and in some cases, betray Him.

The truth is, greatness isn't found in worldly success; it's found in sacrifice. Holiness looks like humility, and love isn't a feeling; it's a choice to serve even when it hurts. Let me be clear: You are royalty. But in this Kingdom, crowns are hidden under towels, and greatness looks a lot like kneeling. This is not a book for the faint of heart. It will challenge your pride, confront your comfort, and call you higher—by calling you lower.

A King Washes Feet isn't just theology; it's an invitation into transformation. I propose that it's time we stop waiting for a move of God and become one. The question is, Will we just admire Him, or will we follow Him?

So go ahead . . . get low. Grab the towel. And wash the world in His love.

Kris Vallotton
senior associate leader, Bethel Church, Redding, CA;
co-founder, Bethel School of Supernatural Ministry;
author of fifteen books, including *The Supernatural Ways of Royalty*, *Spiritual Intelligence*, and *Deliver Us from Evil*

Foreword

I remember the first conversation I ever had with Jessica. Within moments I knew—this is someone who walks closely with Jesus. That depth of love was unmistakable. Over the years, I have had the joy of working with her across Australia and around the world. I have seen her speak to crowds with boldness and minister one-on-one with gentleness. I also get to co-host a podcast with her, where her passion for Christ shows up week after week. It is honest, consistent, and deeply compelling.

That same heart underpins every chapter of this book.

A King Washes Feet is not a comfortable read, and it is not meant to be. This is a book that calls us beyond "comfortable faith" and into the hard and holy work of love. It shines a light on the kind of God we follow. A God who does not just lead with power but bends low to serve. A God who is not afraid of the mess or the pain or the people others avoid. A God who chooses the basin and towel.

One of the most powerful truths this book reminds us of is that strength in the Christian life does not always look like winning or leading. Often it looks like surrender. Real strength is found when we allow ourselves to be vulnerable before God—when we stop trying to fix or hide and simply let Him love us. That is where renewal begins. That is where healing starts.

This book is filled with moments that press gently but firmly on the heart. It will challenge you to look at Jesus differently. It will invite you to see others with more mercy. And it may leave you asking how far you are really willing to go in order to love as He loves.

I had the privilege of watching this message unfold live during our mission across India. Night after night, the theme of footwashing was not just spoken—it was lived. Young people came forward. Their feet were washed by priests and bishops. But more than that, their hearts were touched. I too, night after night, was left in tears. These were not symbolic acts. They were real encounters with a God who draws near. That same invitation is here now—in your hands.

If you come to these pages open, they will meet you. If you let the words do their work, you might just find yourself softened, stretched, and awakened. Not by clever insight or polished answers, but by the quiet power of a King who chooses to serve.

So take your time. Read slowly. And let yourself be met.

This is more than a book. It is an invitation to return to the One who kneels.

Let Him love you.

Fr. Rob Galea
Catholic priest, founder of ICON Ministry,
author, musician, and speaker

Introduction

Welcome to the Footwashing Revival

More than anything, I want someone to pick up this book and say, "This is the Jesus I always wanted to know."

If religion hurt you, this book is for you. If you're a Christian, this book is for you. If you used to know God but now He's the last thing you want, this book is for you. And if you don't know Jesus at all—this book is for you.

If you're angry with someone, this book is for you. If you're crushed, disappointed, or hurt, this book is for you. If you're heartbroken, if you've been abused, if you can't forgive your parents or you don't know how to breathe around the anxiety choking you, this book is for you.

If you're an outcast, this book is for you. If you're a celebrity, this book is for you. If you have no idea who you even are, this book is for you.

If there's one thing I hope you take away from this book, it's that there's room on the footwashing stool for you. For everyone. For the people you like, and the people you don't.

Your Guide

I didn't set out to be an authority on the subject of footwashing. I didn't even intend on creating what became the viral *Footwashing Series* artwork. One Valentine's eve I just sat down with my iPad ready to draw and asked

God, "What does it look like to be Your beloved?" and an image of Jesus washing a bride's feet came to mind. A few days later as I stood in my kitchen, images of all different people having their feet washed exploded through my mind. I froze. "Lord, is that You . . . and are You sure?" I asked Him, knowing that some of the images I'd seen were incredibly controversial. After all . . . who wants to see their perceived enemy sitting on the same footwashing stool as them?

Convinced it was the Lord, or at least convinced I'd rather look a fool than risk saying no to God, I began drawing the people I saw. It was as radical, healing, and controversial as I anticipated. But every time I faced resistance over who I drew having their feet washed by Jesus, I became more convinced that there was no one, *no one*, Jesus would turn away from the seat. After all . . . it's not about who's on the seat, it's about Who's washing the feet.

Every person drawn in *The Footwashing Series* represents someone or something I've been personally convicted of first. You see politicians on the seat because I spoke badly of a politician. You see a firefighter on the seat because my heart broke seeing fires sweep through Los Angeles. You see Judas on the seat because I needed to see my own enemies on the seat.

Even though digital artwork is the way God has used me, I don't consider myself an artist. *Evangelist* or *missionary* resonates more easily, and throughout these pages I'll take you with me into bars, onto stages, and around the world in pursuit of the One Thing worth giving everything up and going anywhere for. But something I love about this digital artwork is that it goes through doors I never could. It arrives into the phones and homes of celebrities, people in closed nations, adult entertainment workers, people of other faiths, prisons, hospitals, everywhere. Jesus will stop at nothing to pursue the one He is on a rescue mission for.

Footwashing Then, Footwashing Now

On the last night of His life, Jesus interrupted the Last Supper—HIS last supper—to kneel and wash the feet of His disciples while they argued over which of them was the greatest. That's not how I would choose to spend the last night of my life, but I have a lot to learn from Jesus about what it looks like to be a king.

We've lost how impactful Jesus' washing feet really was, after reducing footwashing to watching a church leader kneel once a year on carpeted sanctuary floors to pour a splash of water and dab pre-pedicured, spotless feet. Holy Thursday footwashing services involve carefully curated people with token diversity of age, ethnicity, gender, ability, economic status, and holiness.

We're fools if we think footwashing is just a nice symbolic act from two thousand years ago. But we're heretics if we think our footwashing obligation is fulfilled by remembering it once a year at Easter or by watching someone else wash feet. After He got up from washing our own dirty feet, Jesus asked us to wash each other's feet too, and that instruction hasn't expired.

Footwashing is just as relevant today as it was when Jesus' own feet walked the earth. More than an obligation to be fulfilled, footwashing genuinely carries answers to the real things we wrestle with in life, from identity to cancel culture, racism to human relationships. It will be rare, if ever, that we'll have the chance to *physically* wash someone's feet, but we have opportunities every day to metaphorically wash feet. We pick up rocks or kneel with a basin by the way we engage with strangers, family, friends, and enemies.

> "Then the righteous will answer him, 'Lord, when did we see you hungry and feed you, or thirsty and give you something to drink? When did we see you a stranger and invite you in, or needing clothes and clothe you? When did we see you sick or in prison and go to visit you?'
>
> "The King will reply, 'Truly I tell you, whatever you did for one of the least of these brothers and sisters of mine, you did for me.'"
>
> Matthew 25:37–40 NIV

This book is titled *A King Washes Feet* because Jesus is the ultimate King who gave us the first example of washing feet. He presented a new kind of leadership—of kingship.

> "Do nothing from selfishness or conceit, but in humility count others better than yourselves. Let each of you look not only to his own interests,

Introduction

but also to the interests of others. Have this mind among yourselves, which was in Christ Jesus, who, through he was in the form of God, did not count equality with God a thing to be grasped, but emptied himself, taking the form of a servant, being born in the likeness of men."

Philippians 2:3–7

We, as co-heirs of His inheritance and authority, are also called to live a life of royal identity as God's sons and daughters (Romans 8:15–17). Like Jesus, we are meant to live out this royal identity by washing feet.

Book Roadmap

This book isn't gentle. I hope the Jesus on these pages cuts us open and convicts us, and I hope the Jesus inside these pages heals us. Sometimes this book will feel like you're being held so tightly in the arms of Jesus that a broken piece of you gets put back together. Other times, it might feel like you're being convicted. But love is both of these things. In the fictional world of Narnia, author C. S. Lewis describes the lion Aslan (representing Jesus) as not being safe, but good. There's a taste of that lion, that King, in these pages. It's not a safe book, but the Jesus you'll meet inside is overwhelmingly, unfailingly, shockingly Good.

A King Washes Feet is a journey through four main sections: **JESUS, YOU, FRIENDS,** and **ENEMIES.** You can binge the whole book in one big chunk, use the forty short chapters as a daily companion during seasons like Lent, or take your time absorbing the invitation for an encounter with Jesus in every word, Scripture, scribbled note, question, and piece of art found within these pages. Don't rush past the questions in italic throughout the book—these could be the very way God flips your heart over, like Jesus flipped the tables in the temple. I hope my handwritten notes around Scriptures encourage you to dive in and discover what the Lord is speaking to you through His Word too.

Jesus

The first section, **JESUS,** launches us straight into the chaos of Holy Week—the events surrounding Easter. Get covered in Mary's alabaster

Introduction

jar of perfume as she pours it on Jesus' feet, feel Peter's struggle to let his beloved Master wash his filthy feet, and weep over the empty footwashing scene as Jesus lies dead in the tomb we buried Him in.

You

Understanding what Jesus radically did sends us straight into the **YOU** chapters—what it means for us in today's culture. How can we let Jesus wash our dirty feet from the places we've walked and things we've experienced today? How can we sit down after what we've endured, or how unworthy we feel? Feel the water run over your feet as you finally sit down on the stool for yourself, maybe after years of running. He would interrupt a hundred "last suppers" or good plans for an opportunity to minister to you.

Friends

Once you've experienced footwashing for yourself, it's time to do as Jesus asked and begin washing the feet of the people around you, explored through the **FRIENDS** section. Come with me into youth prisons, meet celebrities, and realize who's missing from our pews.

Enemies

And finally . . . just as Jesus washed the feet of Judas, it's time for us to figure out how to bravely and humbly wash the feet of the very people who have hurt, disappointed, and betrayed us too in the **ENEMIES** chapters. You won't walk away the same after realizing who you need to see on the seat.

Footwashing isn't for the fainthearted. That empty stool in front of where Jesus is kneeling with the basin of water will reveal who you think you are, who you think He is, and what you think His blood is strong enough for.

The world is hungry for footwashing. I've seen the theme of footwashing go viral on social media, be shown during the Super Bowl, and light up Times Square. Maybe this is an "easier" Jesus for people to respond to, but it's not a new one. *The Footwashing Series* is radical because what Jesus did and still does is radical. Maybe we've just forgotten, but we're remembering, and I hope this book is another tool that leads to humanity being captivated by a King who washes feet.

Introduction

Washing Feet in India

I didn't know what I was signing up for when Father Rob Galea invited me to join him for his "Something About You" music tour across India. I'd done ministry, I'd been on mission trips, but a tour . . . ? Completely new to me.

Father Rob invited me to join his team for the tour because he was familiar with my *Footwashing Series* artwork. Halfway through the concert, I walked on stage and spoke about Jesus washing feet, and then each night a different young person would have their feet washed by a bishop or priest.

One night the young woman whose feet were washed came down off the stage, visibly emotional, and said, "Something really happened up there. Something is different." Another night a young person openly sobbed while a bishop washed her feet. Twice, visually impaired young people were selected, and one of those nights the room of 1,500 people spontaneously erupted into clapping and cheering after the footwashing. Before one of the concerts began, I walked out of a bathroom stall and found a young woman awkwardly trying to scrub her feet in the bathroom sink. I laughed as I realized quickly who she was and what was going on. "I didn't know I was going to be invited to do this!" she said wryly as she tried to clean her feet before going on stage to have her feet washed.

God did something different and special in every person, every night. I knew He was handpicking each person for a reason, and it wasn't just an act to inspire a stadium full of people—instead, a stadium full of people were witnessing a real encounter someone was having with Jesus. Across those seven concerts throughout India, approximately 20,000 people were reminded that Jesus washed feet, and that He still asks us to do the same.

Welcome to the footwashing revival. Pick up this book and put down the rocks we use to stone people—it's time to wash feet.

Jesus

This Jesus we see washing feet—this is not a new Jesus. This is the original. Get crushed in the frantic crowd welcoming a King on Palm Sunday, see the pieces of the alabaster jar broken open over Jesus' feet, taste the tension radiating from Judas, let your clothes smell of smoke from the charcoal fire as you stand with Peter, feel droplets of water splash onto your arm as you crouch by Jesus as He washes feet. We have to start with the events surrounding the original footwashing story to understand how to respond to it—and to Jesus—today.

ONE

A King in a Crowd

God didn't demand glory . . . He washed feet.

Footwashing isn't over. It is not complete, outdated, or redundant. It didn't start and end during the Last Supper as Jesus washed the feet of His disciples. There is still a seat available today for you, your friends, and your enemies. But until we're brought to our knees by a revelation of what Jesus originally did for us and asked of us, we won't understand why we should get on our knees and wash feet either. This is why we are beginning with Jesus' entry into Jerusalem on Palm Sunday and continuing through key moments surrounding Easter. It is walking down these roads, stepping into these rooms, and sitting inside that tomb with Him that help us understand how unreasonable what Jesus did really was, and how inseparable footwashing is from every area of Jesus' ministry and identity. We are following in the footsteps of a King who washes feet.

Ask yourself:

Do I know the King who washes feet? Am I prepared to wash feet?
Do I believe I have anything to learn from a King who washes feet?

The Chaos of Palm Sunday

The worst crowd I've ever been a part of was in Portugal during the summer of 2023. The heat was stifling thanks to a 100-degree heat wave at exactly the wrong time, as 1.5 million young people gathered in Lisbon for a week to pray alongside Pope Francis at a global gathering called World Youth Day.

"The Pope is arriving!" I dashed through the crowd and caught my first-ever in-person glimpse of Pope Francis in the iconic white Popemobile, accompanied by a strange wave of emotion.

The pilgrimage to the outdoor overnight vigil leading into the final mass of the week together was . . . insane. Everyone wanted to be there, gathered in the name of Jesus, but I won't forget walking for hours in the relentless heat of the day without a cloud in the sky. I saw multiple young people passed out from the ruthless combination of heat and the crush of the crowds. It was twenty-four hours of being constantly pushed and touched and having people in my space. I had never stopped to wonder what a crowd of 1.5 million people would sound like—it was a constant babbling noise without a lull for a single second, all through the night. The introvert in me was well and truly dead inside.

And yet . . . there was this one holy moment that made all the overwhelming noise and crush worth it. As night fell, the entire encampment knelt and silently worshiped God for a few minutes. You could have heard a pin drop. It was one of the most holy moments I've ever experienced. Everything came to a standstill as 1.5 million youth paused everything to adore the King, acknowledge His Presence, put Him as the First Thing.

This is the closest thing I can envision to what we now call Palm Sunday. It's unknown how big the crowd was, but respected Jewish priest, scholar, and historian Josephus recorded that three million Jews filled Jerusalem for the same Passover festival in the year 65 CE.[1]

Massive, pushing crowds lined the streets and yelled for Jesus. People tore branches from palm trees as they shouted, "Hosanna! Blessed is he who comes in the name of the Lord, even the King of Israel!" (John 12:13). Cloaks were spread on the ground in honor of a king (2 Kings 9:13). Jesus rode into Jerusalem, sitting on a young donkey, fulfilling the prophecy in Zechariah 9:9 that the king would come riding on a donkey colt (John 12:14–15). It must have been absolute bedlam on the streets of Jerusalem as the crowds who had heard that Jesus had raised Lazarus from the dead welcomed Jesus as their king.

> "The crowd that had been with him when he called Lazarus out of the tomb and raised him from the dead bore witness. The reason why the crowd went to meet him was that they heard he had done this sign. The Pharisees then said to one another, 'You see that you can do nothing; look, the world has gone after him.'"
>
> John 12:17–19

[Handwritten note: YES, LORD!! WE ARE STILL CAPTIVATED BY YOU]

A Humble King

With the streets of Jerusalem full of people welcoming Jesus as their king, Jesus had every ability to demand glory. It's a vast turnaround from the previous years, when He was almost stoned to death and called a heretic. Our King Jesus was finally the recipient of the glory and honor He deserved. And how did He respond? He didn't request riches, or worship, or fine robes. No—yet again He stepped from His rightful throne to serve us. He got off His humble donkey, another sign of peace and kingship (donkeys were ridden by nonmilitary personnel, and Solomon rode on a mule when his father David commissioned him as the king of Israel in 1 Kings 1:32–40), and a few days later, literally washed feet.

> "'Knowing that He came from God, and went to God,' and that even when He was kneeling there before these men, 'the Father had given all things into His hands,' what did He do? Triumph? Show His majesty? Flash His power? Demand service? 'Girded Himself with a towel and washed His disciples' feet!'"[2]
>
> Alexander MacLaren

Jesus chose a humble donkey to ride in on, feet almost dragging on the ground, instead of a tall, regal horse. How often do I approach people on a strong horse (with intimidation) instead of a humble donkey (with peace)?

TWO

The Servant King

Missing the Messiah

Have you ever missed a moment with God because you were expecting Him to show up one way but He came in another? Maybe you were listening for a big, booming voice, but He was speaking through flowers. Or you were watching for waves to part, but He was touching your face through the hands of a baby you held.

The Jews were waiting for their Messiah. God had sent the prophets, the foreshadowing figures of Jesus, the Scriptures. The priests studied and prepared for the coming of the Lord. And yet when He came, most of the Jewish leaders completely missed Him because He wasn't what they were looking for. They let their own preconceived ideas and expectations rob them of recognizing their Messiah. They had interpreted the Scriptures and the words of the prophets to create an image of the kind of Messiah they wanted, a war hero. Someone to free them from their oppression in the earthly world. A leader to wipe out their physical enemy and give them freedom through a military victory.

They certainly weren't looking for a baby, or a God who acted like a servant.

What kind of God am I looking for? Which aspects of God am I missing because of the box I've put Him in?

It's easy to look at the Jewish leaders and judge them for not recognizing the very Messiah they were waiting for when He was right in front of their faces. In retrospect, it seems so obvious. But I'm not completely convinced I would have easily recognized Him either, because the way He came was offensive and strange. It involved a scandalous pregnancy that should have ended in death, a stable instead of a palace, and the King of the universe beginning His time on earth as a "blob of tissue cells" in the uterus of a girl.

The Messiah's unexpected form didn't start and stop with the hectic circumstances of His entrance into the world. Instead of a warrior, He came as a defenseless child who was at risk of being assassinated, and the pattern continued as He broke out of the box of what people expected of their Messiah. He flipped tables in the temple, condemned the practices of the religious leaders, healed ("worked") on the Sabbath, raised the dead, interacted with women and children, and taught that God was interested in Gentiles (the enemy) not just Jews (the chosen people). And piled on top of all that, this Messiah came "not to be served but to serve" (Matthew 20:28). Jesus wasn't just a radical king interrupting culture and religion, but a *servant* king.

> "But Jesus called them to him and said, 'You know that the rulers of the Gentiles lord it over them, and their great men exercise authority over them. It shall not be so among you; but whoever would be great among you must be your servant, and whoever would be first among you must be your slave; even as the Son of man came not to be served but to serve, and to give his life as a ransom for many.'"
>
> Matthew 20:25–28

Kingship Looks Like Servanthood

The concept of loving and serving to an unusual degree continues to set Christians apart today in a "What can you do for me?" society. It is the backward math of the kingdom—where love looks like sacrifice, someone else paid our debt but we receive His reward, and leadership looks like going low and serving. Peter's refusal to let Jesus wash his feet gives us a clue of just how radical Jesus' actions and teachings were.

> "So the last will be first, and the first will be last."
> Matthew 20:16

Does the concept of God as a servant sit well with me? Do I know Jesus, the King who washes feet?

Jesus' parables, like choosing a lower seat at a banquet table (Luke 14:8–11), repeatedly gave more insight into the importance of going low instead of reaching higher in the kingdom. These parables teach us all to go low and put others before ourselves out of *honor*, not low self-esteem.

Not an Act

Jesus didn't merely give the image of being a servant king. He knelt and took the position of the lowest slave in a household, serving his friends, who rightfully should have been serving *Him*, while during the meal the disciples fought over which of them was the greatest.

> "A dispute also arose among them, which of them was to be regarded as the greatest."
> Luke 22:24

Jesus' act of washing feet was a real-life parable. He wasn't exchanging the form of God for one of a servant—He was *revealing* the true form of God. A Servant King.

What we sometimes miss is that after Jesus got up from where He knelt to wash feet, He said to the disciples,

> "If I then, your Lord and Teacher, have washed your feet, you also ought to wash one another's feet. For I have given you an example, that you also should do as I have done to you."
>
> John 13:14–15

IT'S MY TURN

Jesus calls us to this ministry of washing feet too, and it's time for a footwashing revival. I've seen the theme of footwashing everywhere, from commercials during the Super Bowl to viral artwork on social media, from billboards in Times Square to tours in India. Because we are not "greater than our master" (cf. John 13:16), we are also called to humbly serve and love people like our Servant King.

THREE

More Radical Than We Think

Dinner with Dirty Feet

While I was in India as a part of Father Rob's Christian concert tour, I wore Birkenstock sandals (the classic "Jesus sandals") as it was too hot for closed-in shoes. I remember walking onto the stage to talk about footwashing during one of the concerts at the end of a particularly long day, so aware of how filthy my feet were. If you'd swabbed the brown film covering my feet as I stood on the stage, I have no doubt the results would have shown—at the very minimum—traces of dirt, sweat, insect repellent, urine (I had not mastered the very basic toilet facilities), and animal excrement. Standing on the stage that night, I tried not to laugh as I talked about the metaphor of letting Jesus wash your dirty feet, knowing mine were literally disgusting and I was a living example of exactly what I was trying to communicate. I understood why the first duty of a Jewish host[1] was to have their lowest-ranking servant provide water for a guest to wash their feet as they walked in the door.[2]

Given that Jesus was the one to eventually wash their feet, it's possible that no one had washed their feet when the disciples gathered for the Last Supper. If the disciples' feet were anything like mine that day in India, I have no doubt that even Jesus' feet would have been ruining the meal as they gathered around a low table to eat.

The Master/Student Dynamic

In Jewish culture, a teacher had no right to ask his students to wash his feet. It would have been considered an exploitation of the relationship. What Jesus did as the *Master* washing the feet of his students wasn't just an unexpected service, but culturally shocking. It would have been uncalled for if the disciples had washed Jesus' feet as His students, but it was unthinkable for the Master to kneel and perform the disgusting work of the least-respected household servant and wash the feet of his students.[3]

> *Would I have kept following a leader whose behavior was culturally inappropriate?*

Remember that washing the feet of guests as they entered a house was the job of the servant with the lowest rank. Jesus didn't just do a job someone else could have done but didn't bother to do; He did something it was culturally wrong to do. He looked at the line that separated ranks of people and firmly stepped over it. The guest of honor served like a slave.

How to Approach a King

Even beyond the appropriate boundaries between a teacher and student, it was forbidden to approach a king or prince without proper preparation, which included washing the hands and feet.[4] Under Mosaic Law, the Lord instructed Moses to prepare a bronze basin which priests were required to wash their hands and feet in before approaching the tent of meeting and the altar. If they didn't wash their hands and feet before approaching the altar, the consequence was death.

SHOW HONOR TO THE LORD

> "The LORD said to Moses, 'You shall also make a laver of bronze, with its base of bronze, for washing. . . . They shall wash their hands and their feet, lest they die: it shall be a statute for ever to them, even to him and to his descendants throughout their generations.'"
>
> Exodus 30:17–18, 21

The disciples had recognized Jesus as the King and Messiah as He rode into Jerusalem on a donkey days earlier, but if they'd walked into the house without washing their feet, they hadn't shown respect by presenting themselves in a way which honored His royal identity. They would have appeared dirty and unwashed in His presence. It was inappropriate for them to show up dirty . . . it was ridiculous that the King they should have cleaned up for ended up cleaning *them*.

How often does overfamiliarity with Jesus make me abuse His friendship and fail to treat Him with the respect He deserves?

The Bridegroom and the Bride

In rabbinical literature, the wife was responsible for serving her husband by washing his face and feet each day, no matter how many maids she may have had, as gestures of affection toward her husband.[5]

This is a powerful illustration of the Bride of Christ missing an opportunity to wash Christ the Bridegroom's feet. As individuals, the disciples ignored both their responsibility and the opportunity to serve Jesus and show love toward Him by washing His feet, content for someone else to offer to do it. Overfamiliarity toward Jesus stole something from Him that He was worthy of.

How is it that despite all of the ways the disciples abused their relationship with Jesus, their King and God, *He* was the one who broke all the traditions and knelt and washed *their* feet as if they were the kings, not the very people disrespecting Him. It makes me want to cry.

FOUR

Too Much and Not Enough

I resonate with Simon Peter over and over in the Gospels. He is a completely relatable and honest figure in the way he interacts with Jesus. He is so *human*, and notably a work in progress. Peter is a prophetic picture—even a promise—that Jesus doesn't abandon us when we mess up or misunderstand Him repeatedly. God won't ever give up on us.

Peter's Refusal

When Jesus began to wash the disciples' feet, Peter initially tried to refuse. He saw Jesus as a king but not necessarily a servant king. Read the following passage carefully; look for the two moments that Peter tries to tell Jesus (again—a bit of a theme with Peter—see Matthew 16:22) that he knows better than Him.

> "Then he poured water into a basin, and began to wash the disciples' feet, and to wipe them with the towel with which he was girded. He came to Simon Peter; and Peter said to him, 'Lord, do you wash my feet?' Jesus answered him, 'What I am doing you do not know now, but afterward you will understand.' Peter said to him, 'You shall never wash my feet.' *"TOO MUCH"* Jesus answered him, "If I do not wash you, you have no part in

me.' Simon Peter said to him, 'Lord, not my feet only but also my hands and my head!'"

"NOT ENOUGH"

John 13:5–9

Peter's misunderstanding of the character of God leads him to tell Jesus, his Master, that he both does too much ("You shall never wash my feet") and then not enough ("Lord, not my feet only but also my hands and my head!").[1]

> *Do I ever think I know better than God? How many times have I tried to tell Him I have a better plan, or He just needs to adjust His to fit mine?*

Healthy Leaders Serve and Let Themselves Be Served

The mark of a truly servant-hearted leader is the ability not just to serve, but to be served. If we refuse to let others serve us, it can stem from a hidden pride. Jesus, as the healthiest leader to exist, knew how to both give and receive. He allowed Mary to pour her perfume on His feet even when others were wildly offended by this action, and then days later He knelt and washed the feet of the same disciples who were offended by Mary's honor. And guess what? They were still offended. They were offended by the way Jesus received, and they were offended by the way Jesus gave. People think that only Judas was offended by Mary's actions, but the Gospel of Matthew records that *the disciples* were indignant.

NOT JUST JUDAS!

> "But when the disciples saw it, they were indignant, saying, 'Why this waste? For this ointment might have been sold for a large sum, and given to the poor.'"
>
> Matthew 26:8–9

Over and over again, misunderstanding the nature of God leads to the disciples' protestations.

When we have a right perspective of Jesus, we understand our need to have Him wash our feet.

> "Peter said to him, 'You shall never wash my feet.' Jesus answered him, 'If I do not wash you, you have no part in me.'"
>
> John 13:8

Jesus makes one thing very clear: Footwashing is not optional.

Peter fails to initially realize that he is in need of what Jesus is doing. It is not something Peter could earn, but something he had to humble himself to receive from Jesus. Yes, having the King serve you is challenging, but our refusal to sit on the footwashing stool and let Jesus wash our feet could cost us everything.

It is not enough for us to serve Jesus, work to advance the kingdom, or even participate in the miraculous. Peter preached the gospel, cast out demons, saw Jesus transfigured in His glory next to Elijah and Moses, and even walked on water himself—but without posturing his heart to receive a spiritual cleansing from Jesus, it wouldn't have been sufficient to save him. Judas allowed Jesus to wash his feet physically, but not spiritually. Despite both Peter and Judas betraying Jesus the next day in some way, it was Peter's desire to receive what Jesus offered that saved him. The literal footwashing is not the crucial part here—it is the spiritual element of it.

> "It is not the area of skin that is washed that matters but the acceptance of Jesus' lowly service."[2]
>
> Leon Morris

I do not want to be Peter, protesting and too prideful to sit down and receive what Jesus is freely offering me. I don't have to earn it. I don't have to unlock a particular level of holiness. I don't have to be a theological or scriptural expert. I don't have to save a certain number of souls. I don't have to cast out demons or even walk on water. All I must do is humble myself enough to sit down and receive.

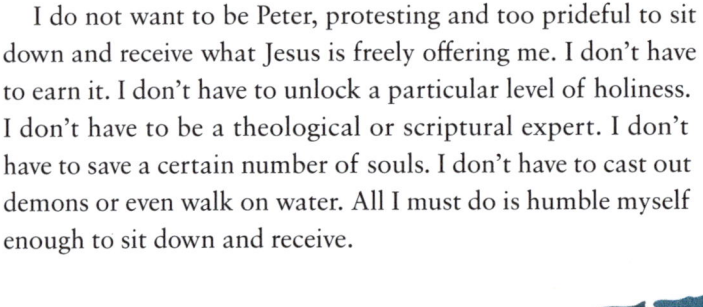

FIVE

Unworthy

Surviving an Earthquake

There's no good age to experience a traumatic event, but seventeen is young to discover what is inside of you when you think you're about to die.

On February 22, 2011, a catastrophic 6.3 magnitude earthquake in New Zealand killed 185 people and injured over 7,000 others as buildings collapsed. I'll never forget trying to crawl under a desk and being thrown around at more than the force of gravity (1.51g) as the multistory building I worked at in the heart of the city slanted sideways and I heard the unbelievably deafening sound of buildings collapsing around ours. I knew I might die, and the only thing that came out of me was a repetitive scream: "GOD! GOD! HELP, GOD!" You never really know what's inside of you until you're put in a position for something to come out.

I met and gave my life to God at age eleven, and at seventeen God was my friend, but my life wasn't massively centered around Him just yet. So what—or Who—I screamed for was a surprise to me. By watching the news, reading history books, or even musing on past stressful situations in my life, I could have made an educated guess as to my hypothetical response to the danger of a life-threatening earthquake. I would have expected myself to be a stand-and-fight kind of a girl, relying on my own wits to survive—I never would have expected that I would scream for God.

Discovering What Was Inside Peter

I can only imagine the shame the apostle Peter felt when he was faced with the moment that for three years he'd been preparing for (the Romans arresting and killing his Teacher and friend). Instead of love and courage, fear came out of him. He's recorded as being bold (Acts 4:13), but when Jesus was arrested, tried, and put to death, Peter hid and denied Him. Fear didn't win only the first time, either, or even when he faced the same question a second time, but *three miserable times* fear was his response instead of love and courage.

> *How many times have I been faced with a familiar situation, a fresh opportunity to choose better, and I let fear win over and over again in my life?*

We might be a mystery to ourselves, but we are not a mystery to God.

> "You have searched me, Lord, [YOU KNOW EVERYTHING ABOUT ME]
> and you know me.
> You know when I sit and when I rise;
> you perceive my thoughts from afar.
> You discern my going out and my lying down;
> you are familiar with all my ways.
> Before a word is on my tongue
> you, Lord, know it completely."
>
> Psalm 139:1–4 NIV

[AND STILL LOVE + CHOOSE ME]

[*REMINDS ME OF THE SONG "YOU KNOW ME" BY BETHEL MUSIC + STEFFANY GRETZINGER]

The night before Jesus was arrested, He knelt and washed the feet of Peter and told Peter that he would deny Him three times (Luke 22:31–34). Jesus knew all along that not just Judas, but Peter too would deny him.

Since the beginning of time God has pursued relationship with us regardless of the possibility of rejection, exploitation, or betrayal. Jesus knew Peter would deny Him three times, but He didn't reject him in advance, condemn him, shame him, or send him away. He didn't build a single brick of separation in the name of self-protection. No, Jesus reassured Peter that He knew him and still wanted and loved him. He washed his feet. It was a gesture that built *more* intimacy. Jesus didn't step away from Peter, He stepped toward him.

> "And the Lord turned and looked at Peter. And Peter remembered the word of the Lord, how he had said to him, 'Before the cock crows today, you will deny me three times.' And he went out and wept bitterly."
>
> Luke 22:61–62

In the worst way, in the worst circumstances possible, Peter found out what was inside himself. It wasn't what he expected, but it wasn't unexpected to Jesus. Our Maker and Friend knows what's inside of us, even when it's a mystery to ourselves. Peter needed to have his feet washed by Jesus—a sign of His love, His forgiveness, His restoration back into relationship. And Jesus had already done this for him ahead of time.

What is in me?

Am I afraid of what's inside of me?

Do I think Jesus has ever been surprised by what's inside of me?

Have I ever been ashamed by what's come out of me?

Which shameful moments do I need Jesus to come and wash my feet over?

Peter's willingness to die for Jesus before Jesus' death was a theory built on emotion. But once Jesus has died for Peter, he became the Rock—willing to die for Jesus because of how Jesus died for Him.[1]

SIX

Barabbas Is Me

Fri 10:14am
This is not meant to be a hostile question but I'm curious, would you draw the line at Hitler?

It wasn't the first time I'd received a message or comment like this in relation to my *Footwashing Series* art, and I'm certain it won't be the last. I believe a question like this is asking something fundamental that actually has nothing to do with a specific person, and everything to do with who the person represents . . . the worst of us. Would Jesus die for the worst of us? Is there a line He would draw? Is His love conditional *at all*? Would Jesus wash the feet of "Hitler" too?

Barabbas—They Chose the Wrong Son

OTHER ANCIENT AUTHORITIES READ "JESUS BARABBAS"

"BAR" = "SON"
"ABBA" = "FATHER"
NAME MEANS "SON OF THE FATHER"

"Now the chief priests and the elders persuaded the people to ask for Barabbas and destroy Jesus. The governor again said to them, 'Which of the two do you want me to release for you?' And they said, 'Barabbas.' Pilate said to them, "Then what shall I do with Jesus who is called Christ?' They all said, 'Let

him be crucified.' And he said, 'Why, what evil has he done?' But they shouted all the more, 'Let him be crucified.'"

"So when Pilate saw that he was gaining nothing, but rather that a riot was beginning, he took water and washed his hands before the crowd, saying, 'I am innocent of this righteous man's blood; see to it yourselves.' And all the people answered, 'His blood be on us and on our children!' Then he released for them Barabbas, and having scourged Jesus, delivered him to be crucified."

I never understood why Barabbas was the one shown mercy and set free from his impending crucifixion instead of Jesus. From an earthly perspective, Barabbas *was* guilty of something, and Jesus was innocent. It was the day of the Passover feast, and this is why Pilate offered to free one of the prisoners from "death row." Freeing a prisoner was a Passover custom intended to honor the night that Pharaoh's firstborn son died so that God's firstborn son Israel could be released.[1] On the day of Atonement in the Jewish year, the high priest would cast lots over two goats—one was sacrificed, and the other went free (Leviticus 16). The priest would place his hands with the blood of the sacrificed goat on the head of the living goat and confess the sins of the people of Israel. As it was released into the wilderness, it would symbolically carry away the sins of the nation.

Scapegoat

On Good Friday, Pilate "examined" Jesus in the way a high priest would examine a goat for any imperfections and found him faultless. Jesus' blood at Calvary became the permanent fulfillment of the Day of Atonement. Jesus was the perfect sacrifice, and meanwhile Barabbas was set free.

Barabbas and Jesus[2]

Barabbas	Jesus
His name is Jesus Barabbas—"Jesus, son of the father" ("Bar" = "son" and "Abba" = "father")	Jesus is the Son of the Father
Murderer—takes lives	Gives His life
Insurrectionist—wants to overthrow the king	Accused of insurrection—but is the rightful King who dies for those who rebel against Him
Guilty of his crimes but will be set free	Innocent of crime but will die for the sin of others

Jesus is the real Son of the Father. He's innocent but will die even though the other man holds all the guilt. Jesus will take Barabbas's punishment. In other words . . . the Jews freed the wrong son.[3]

It all feels so horribly wrong, until you realize one thing.

Setting Barabbas free makes no sense until you realize that Barabbas is me.

Have I made this realization before? Does it change how I understand the Passion narrative?

We are the ones who are guilty, and Jesus took our place. The one who was innocent took my place. It would have been fair for me to "go to the cross"—I *was* guilty. But Jesus dragged my cross. Jesus died my death. Jesus lay in my grave.

As Jesus took Barabbas's place, He made it clear once again that He was paying for all of our crimes, and He wasn't going to leave a single person behind.

Did Jesus Die to Atone for All, or Not?

When Jesus took Barabbas's place, the place of a convicted murderer on death row, He made it clear that His blood being spilled was for everyone. Let's go back to the Day of Atonement outlined in Leviticus 16, where under the Old Covenant the high priest would cast lots over two goats. One was sacrificed and the other symbolically carried away the people's sin into the wilderness. Jesus was the perfect New Covenant fulfillment of this. Jesus was both the sacrificial goat, whose blood atoned for sin, and the scapegoat, who carried our sins away permanently. His death fulfilled both roles, making atonement complete under the New Covenant. Jesus wasn't unaware or out of control at any second of the journey to Calvary that unfolded. He told Pontius Pilate that he only had the authority given to him by God. The crowd's decision to free either Jesus or Barabbas wasn't outside of God's control. Jesus chose to take the place of every single one of us, including Barabbas. He didn't leave a single person behind. He took the punishment we all deserved for our various "crimes" (sin).

I propose this is what people are really asking and wrestling with when they ask questions like whether Jesus would wash the feet of someone like Hitler. Jesus took the place of every single one of us, so yes—He died for the "Hitlers" of the world too. If you aren't convinced of that, I'd encourage you to search Scripture for answers about who Jesus came and died for.

What do I believe? Do I believe Jesus died for everyone?

The point I'm trying to communicate isn't about Hitler, or to justify his horrific crimes. He's an example of a person like Barabbas—that Jesus would take the place of the worst of us. That Barabbas is really me.

Asking "Would Jesus wash Hitler's feet?" is the wrong question. What we should really ask is, "Was Jesus' blood enough to cover everyone?"

SEVEN

We Killed God

A crucifix—Jesus' tortured body hanging on a cross—symbolizes real love, even though it's something you want to look away from. It is ugly and uncomfortable. A person in the middle of dying. What a horrendous piece of jewelry to wear, unless it means something beyond torture.

When I look at a crucifix, what do I see? Have I grown numb to the scandal of the cross?

> "This is my commandment, that you love one another as I have loved you. Greater love has no man than this, that a man lay down his life for his friends."
>
> John 15:12–13

There is someone who died for you. You were sentenced to die as a punishment for your sins, but Jesus stepped forward and volunteered to die in your place. He suffered and then had His life ended instead of yours. The nails that should have gone in your hands went through His hands instead.

Jesus' cry of "My God, my God, why hast thou forsaken me?" (Mark 15:34) is the first line of Psalm 22, which the Jewish people were familiar with, prophesying the way the Messiah would die. Right until His last breaths, He was trying to reach out to the very people who had crucified Him, to give hope to His friends who had failed so miserably on this final day with Him.

Jesus

[handwritten: JESUS CRIED OUT THESE WORDS — A REMINDER OF THIS PSALM]

[circled:] "My God, my God, why has thou forsaken me?
Why art thou so far from helping me, from the words of my groaning? . . .
I am poured out like water,
and all my bones are out of joint. . . . *[handwritten: CRUCIFIXION OFTEN CAUSED DISLOCATION]*
[handwritten: A TERM USED FOR ROMANS →] Yea, [circled: dogs] are round about me;
a company of evildoers encircle me;
they have pierced my hands and feet— *[handwritten: NAILED TO THE CROSS]*
I can count all my bones—
[handwritten: MT 15:26-27] they stare and gloat over me;
they divide my garments among them,
and for my raiment they cast lots."

[handwritten: THEY CAST LOTS FOR HIS GARMENTS]

Psalm 22:1, 14, 16–18

[handwritten: WHAT WE DID TO HIM WAS TERRIBLE.]

There's no doubt; we killed God. We killed the only one who could wash our feet.

How Did We Repay Him?

When she was an outcast at the well, He brought her in.
When his friends lowered him down through the roof, He healed him.
When his child died, He brought her back to life.
When she was tormented, He called her name and set her free.
When they had no food, He fed them all and sent them away with extra.
When he had already sold Him for thirty silver coins, He washed his feet anyway.
And how did we repay Him?
We sold Him out for a pitiful amount, not that we could ever put a price on the life of God anyway. Maybe it was better not to try?

We shredded the skin on His back thirty-nine times. Forty was known to kill a man, so we went one less, just to be sure He survived so we could kill Him another bloody way.

We pressed a crown of thorns onto His head, making blood run down His face like it already had the night before as He agonized over knowing what was to come and decided we were worth it still. It rather takes the satisfaction out of the kill when your victim is the one who decided to let you kill Him, don't you think?

We stripped Him naked and hung Him totally vulnerable, like a thief, as if He would ever hold anything back or take anything we didn't want to give anyway.

We knocked metal nails through His hands and pinned Him to the wood of a tree His hands created, as if anything but love was holding Him there.

That's how I repaid him for every kindness He ever showed me. How I repaid Him for the time He stopped others from stoning me, the time He stopped in a crowd because His eyes sought out just me, the table He set and invited me to when no one else would acknowledge I existed.

It's a grim picture, and I'm lying to myself if I think my name isn't signed on His death certificate too.

We pulled His dead body from the cross and put His corpse inside a tomb and sealed it permanently. Left God to rot alone.

With Jesus dead, there is no one to wash our feet. There is no one to rescue us from the valley of the shadow of death. There is no one to heal our crippling pain. There is no one to set us free from tormenting dreams.

There is no one to save our children. There is no cure for our sickness, no one to receive us when our friends lower us down through the roof. There is no hope.

He is dead. The only one who could wash our feet lay cold, still, lifeless, and broken in a pitch-black tomb sealed with rock.

Have I experienced a season where it felt like Jesus was "dead in the tomb" in my life, where I couldn't feel Him or see Him moving?

EIGHT

Scars

I have a new scar on my left foot, but rather than be disappointed by the angry red line marking my skin, I am rather proud of this particular scar.

My personality means that I don't naturally enjoy learning new skills. My tendency toward perfectionism doesn't ordinarily leave room for anything I'm not immediately good at, whether it's learning a new sport or ministry skill or design software. Maybe because of this aspect of my personality, or to keep it in check, I've made a point of setting goals and achieving them. The biggest challenge isn't trying things for the first time—it's keeping going about ten minutes in when I'm not immediately perfect at something. So far I've earned my motorbike license and learned to snowboard (still terrible at it, can't believe I haven't broken a leg). My latest goal: learn to surf.

Given that Australia's waters are infested with sharks, I opted to take a surf lesson while I was in Indonesia. As usual, about ten minutes in the biggest battle wasn't the waves, but convincing myself to stay in the waves

and persevere rather than give up when I struggled to immediately stand up on my board. Two hours later I was catching most of the waves and successfully surfing! I got out of the water and had a deep cut in the side of my foot from some coral I'd accidentally kicked under the water.

All that's left now is a scar. When I look at it, yes, I remember the blood and pain (nothing like having straight alcohol poured onto an open wound as a disinfectant), but more than anything it reminds me of what I achieved—learning to surf even when I wanted to give up. The mark tells a story of achieving something worthy of a scar.

Jesus' Scars

If you looked down today and paid attention to the hands washing your feet, you would see scars on them. Brutal ones. Look further, see the scars on His feet. Down His side runs a scar large enough to put a hand inside. They all tell a story, too, of something infinitely more significant than conquering waves. I look at my scar and remember conquering waves. He looks at His scars, and they tell a story of conquering death.

> "Now Thomas, one of the twelve, called the Twin, was not with them when Jesus came. So the other disciples told him, 'We have seen the Lord.' But he said to them, 'Unless I see in his hands the print of the nails, and place my finger in the mark of the nails, and place my hand in his side, I will not believe.'
>
> "Eight days later, his disciples were again in the house, and Thomas was with them. The doors were shut, but Jesus came and stood among them, and said, 'Peace be with you.' Then he said to Thomas, 'Put your finger here, and see my hands; and put out your hand, and place it in my side; do not be faithless, but believing.' Thomas answered him, 'My Lord and my God!'"
>
> John 20:24–28

[Handwritten annotations: "JESUS' SCARS" pointing to underlined passages; "JESUS' SCARS ARE PROOF OF WHO HE IS — LEAD PEOPLE CLOSER TO HIM"]

Jesus is not ashamed of His scars. He kept them as a reminder to us, as proof of His sacrifice and victory over death. No man should have survived those scars. They yell, "There is a God of the impossible!" The still-current wounds remind us that His blood is still enough. Jesus does not have to die again to cover our sin. The price still counts.

It's these scars that remind us of our freedom. When you sit and have Jesus wash your feet, and see His disfigured hands, I hope those wounds remind you that the price He paid was enough.

When you wonder whether or not Jesus would wash someone's feet, I hope you catch a glimpse of the holes in Jesus' feet, and they remind you He paid a sufficient price to cover their sin too.

Am I ashamed of my own scars, whether literal or figurative?

It's Not About Who's on the Seat

The phrase, "It's not about who's on the seat; it's about Who's washing the feet" came to mind after *The Footwashing Series* launched and I received a lot of pushback about whether I was drawing sacrilegious images because of who I illustrated having their feet washed. (Incidentally, that's one of my biggest fears; I'm terrified of publishing anything that doesn't reflect Jesus rightly.)

Jesus washing feet was never about who was sitting on the seat. If it is, we're placing more weight on someone's sin than we are on the power of His blood.

There's a reason that Peter's refusal to let Jesus wash his feet is an example of what *not* to do—because we need to sit down and receive the free gift Jesus offers us; the one that we all need to respond to. Some of us will receive externally but won't let the washing permeate our hearts, like Judas, and some of us will have a hard time sitting down, like Peter. Ultimately, the scars on the hands doing the washing communicate one thing—I don't get to decide who gets to sit on the seat.

It's not about who's on the seat; it's about Who's washing the feet.

NINE

The Charcoal Fire

There are two very strong figures associated with the betrayal of Jesus. The first is Judas, through the way he sold Jesus to the "enemy," and the other is Peter, by his denial of Jesus three times.

Two men. Two betrayals of Jesus. And two sets of feet He washed the night before. All very similar . . . but with terribly different outcomes. One disciple had his life redeemed, and the other lost his life.

It's a serious and sobering topic, but I can't just skip over it because it's uncomfortable. There's something important for us to learn here, which will help us in our own walk with the Lord.

Judas's Shame

The key difference between the two men is that while one ran toward Jesus, the other ran in the opposite direction. Peter felt his failure deeply, and I can't imagine the shame he experienced, but he ran toward Jesus. Judas, however, let the shame and regret of his betrayal have the final word and ended his life. I feel grieved just writing it.

> *When you experience shame or pain, do you run toward God or away from Him?*

Peter's Restoration

To understand Peter's restoration, we have to look first at his lowest point: his three rejections of Jesus. The Gospel accounts from John and Matthew both hold keys that point to Peter's restoration:

> "The maid who kept the door said to Peter, 'Are not you also one of this man's disciples?' He said, 'I am not.' Now the servants and officers had made a charcoal fire, because it was cold, and they were standing and warming themselves; Peter also was with them, standing and warming himself."
>
> John 18:17–18

NOTE: PAY ATTENTION TO IMAGERY

> "Now Peter was sitting outside in the courtyard. And a maid came up to him, and said, 'You also were with Jesus the Galilean.' But he denied it before them all, saying, 'I do not know what you mean.' And when he went out to the porch, another maid saw him, and she said to the bystanders, 'This man was with Jesus of Nazareth.' And again he denied it with an oath, 'I do not know the man.' After a little while the bystanders came up and said to Peter, 'Certainly you are also one of them, for your accent betrays you.' Then he began to invoke a curse on himself and to swear, 'I do not know the man.' And immediately the cock crowed. And Peter remembered the saying of Jesus, 'Before the cock crows, you will deny me three times.' And he went out and wept bitterly."
>
> Matthew 26:69–75

FIRST DENIAL ①
SECOND DENIAL ②
THIRD DENIAL ③

Peter stands by a charcoal fire and denies Jesus three times. What similarities can you find as Jesus and Peter interact after Jesus' resurrection?

The Charcoal Fire

NOT A CRUEL REPLAY—
A RESTORATION OPPORTUNITY

"When they got out on land, they saw a charcoal fire there, with fish lying on it, and bread. Jesus said to them, 'Bring some of the fish that you have just caught.' So Simon Peter went aboard and hauled the net ashore, full of large fish, a hundred and fifty-three of them; and although there were so many, the net was not torn. Jesus said to them, 'Come and have breakfast.' Now none of the disciples dared ask him, 'Who are you?' They knew it was the Lord. Jesus came and took the bread and gave it to them, and so with the fish. This was now the third time that Jesus was revealed to the disciples after he was raised from the dead.

MAY HAVE REPRESENTED ALL NATIONS AS GREEKS BELIEVED THERE WERE 153 KNOWN SPECIES OF FISH

JESUS CALLED PETER TO BE A FISHER OF PEOPLE

"When they had finished breakfast, Jesus said to Simon Peter, 'Simon, son of John, do you love me more than these?' He said to him, 'Yes, Lord; you know that I love you.' He said to him, 'Feed my lambs.' A second time he said to him, 'Simon, son of John, do you love me?' He said to him, 'Yes, Lord; you know that I love you.' He said to him, 'Tend my sheep.' He said to him the third time, 'Simon, son of John, do you love me?' Peter was grieved because he said to him the third time, 'Do you love me?' And he said to him, 'Lord, you know everything; you know that I love you.' Jesus said to him, 'Feed my sheep. Truly, truly, I say to you, when you were young, you girded yourself and walked where you would; but when you are old, you will stretch out your hands, and another will gird you and carry you where you do not wish to go.' (This he said to show by what death he was to glorify God.) And after this he said to him, 'Follow me.'" → "I STILL CHOOSE YOU."

① FIRST DENIAL REDEEMED

② SECOND DENIAL REDEEMED

③ THIRD DENIAL REDEEMED

"YOUR CALLING HASN'T CHANGED OR BEEN TAKEN AWAY."

John 21:9–19

Here's what stands out to me:

- Jesus recreates a recognizable element from the moment of Peter's betrayal of Him: the charcoal fire. Where Peter once stood by a charcoal fire and denied Jesus, now Peter has an opportunity to be

- with Jesus next to one again. Jesus is so good at redeeming painful situations.
- Peter denied Jesus three times, and Jesus isn't being cruel by asking Peter over and over again whether he loves Him—He's giving Peter a chance to redeem every single one of the three times Peter denied Him.
- Why does Jesus respond with "Feed my lambs," "Tend my sheep," "Feed my sheep"? Because He is reiterating that Peter's calling hasn't changed. Even though what Peter had done should have disqualified him from being a church leader, Jesus told Peter the call on his life hadn't changed. He could mess up, repent, and still be called.
- "Follow me." Jesus ends with these two powerful words. What is Jesus really saying? If you had been Peter, having this conversation after the biggest, most catastrophic failure of your life, what would you really hear Jesus saying to you? "I still choose you."

You might feel as though you've absolutely failed. Maybe it's in a relationship, or your relationship with the Lord. Do you ever look at the Lord, and wonder, *Why would He still want me? Does He still want me? I've failed with everything He's ever put into my hands. He called me and I walked away. He asked me and I said no*. I want you to remember Peter's journey. He messed up repeatedly. He rejected our Lord. And what did Jesus do? He washed away the dirt and the shame from where he failed and said, "I still want you. I still choose you. Nothing has changed about who you're made to be or what you're called to. You aren't disqualified. I forgive you. I love you."

What is the dirt and shame covering my feet? What does God want to redeem in my life as I stand by my charcoal fire?

Don't run from Him; run toward Him. He's exactly what you need to alleviate your guilt, free you from shame, bring you comfort.

You

Understanding what Jesus has done for us makes us want to reach other people with the same love we've encountered. It's why we just spent the first section of this book walking through the original footwashing story in the "Jesus" segment, understanding what Jesus did and how wild it really was. Now we let Jesus wash *our* feet. Welcome to the "You" section.

TEN

Washing the Bride

Washing Feet on Valentine's

In my third and final year of ministry college, a small team and I oversaw a diverse, enthusiastic group of sixty first-year ministry students. Our entire group gathered every Wednesday morning, and one of those weekly meetings happened to fall on February 14. The male students decided they wanted to honor the female students as a surprise, and I wasn't prepared for the level of effort they went to. Men lined the entrance way to the room in suits, some of the younger men swimming in borrowed suits others in the group had loaned them for the occasion. Everywhere I looked, pink balloons and streamers covered the walls. Several men were flipping pancakes and sizzling bacon at a breakfast bar, and throughout the room these wonderful men had set up stations to demonstrate the love of Jesus to women of all ages and life stages. We had 17-year-old single girls, right through to 60-year-old widows.

The station that stood out amongst them all was the quiet one in the middle of the room: footwashing. I watched as women sat down in front of a basin of essential oil–scented water, and young men knelt and tenderly washed their feet as they ministered to them. They quietly reminded the women of their worth, their beauty as they washed. They apologized for the times men hadn't treated them as they should have, and, with words infused with the Holy Spirit, gave them hope for their future relationships and spoke as the Father's voice over them. It was beautiful.

This was a touch, a taste, of the Father's love.

We Need to Let Jesus Wash Our Feet First

What did Jesus do before He instructed His disciples to wash feet? Jesus washed their feet first.

We need to sit down on the stool and let Jesus wash our feet. Don't be like Peter: too proud, or with an underlying sense of false humility, or trying to keep your fist tightly wound around control, telling Jesus what He can or can't do in your life.

Having Jesus wash our feet is an *encounter* with Him, and it's real encounters with God that transform us and change religious behaviors into acts of love. Two people can perform the exact same action of washing feet; one to earn God's love, the other *because* they love God.

Creating *The Footwashing Series*

The Footwashing Series artwork began with the image of a bride having her feet washed, a tangible illustration of what it looks like to be the beloved of God. In the picture, Jesus is kneeling and tenderly washing the feet of an emotional woman in a wedding dress, with a lavish bunch of flowers He gave her lying in her lap.

I shared the image on my small social media platforms, wondering if there was someone else who might need to see how Jesus loves us, His Bride, too. I was in no way prepared when I rolled over and picked up my phone the next morning and discovered more than 27,000 others had resonated with this image. It was the start of what's now the *Footwashing Series*.

The Church, the Bride

> "Husbands, love your wives, as Christ loved the church and gave himself up for her, that he might sanctify her, having cleansed her by the washing of water with the word, that he might present the church to himself in splendor, without spot or wrinkle or any such thing, that she might be holy and without blemish." Ephesians 5:25–27

Washing the Bride

God made covenant with us, the church, His Bride, knowing we would be unfaithful. But despite how many times we were unfaithful to God and abused our covenant with Him—creating idols, worshiping other gods—God never once gave up on us. He didn't withdraw His covenant with us, even when we broke it.

What strikes me so much about the love of Jesus is that He didn't go to the cross with a guarantee that any of us would respond to His love. He risked everything to pursue a restored covenant relationship with us.

In the Bible, the book of Hosea is the prophetic story of a man pursuing and marrying a prostitute named Gomer, of a husband's love and faithfulness toward a wife who was an adulterer. This isn't about Hosea and Gomer; it is a prophetic picture of Jesus and us, His Bride.

Our Bridegroom (Jesus) has the ability to wash us clean and make us a spotless Bride for himself. Without the blood of Jesus, we are walking around in our old rags.

In traditional liturgies, the person being baptized is clothed in a white garment to represent the spiritual cleansing they receive from the Lord as they're washed by the water. It's an element that I believe connects to footwashing: Jesus cleansing His Bride.

You might feel as though you are still walking around in your old rags, or dragging them with you "just in case" you decide to put aside your new white garment and go back to those old, filthy but familiar grave clothes. Here's what I need you to know: The Enemy wants you to carry shame from your past with you every day. But God says He has burned your old rags and clothed you as a daughter or son, with a ring and a robe, and lavished extravagant flowers on you.

> "See what great love the Father has lavished on us, that we should be called children of God! And that is what we are!"
>
> 1 John 3:1 NIV

(handwritten annotation: GENEROUS / EXTRAVAGANT — circling "lavished")

Do I feel like I'm still carrying my old rags? Have I burned my old rags or am I holding on to them just in case one day I go back to them? What would my old rags be?

He is not a God who withholds or only gives us what we need. His gifts toward us, both tangible and intangible, are ridiculously generous.

The Flowers

I first encountered this extravagance of the Father when I spent a year living with a group of religious sisters. Religious sisters (similar to nuns) take three vows—of poverty, chastity, and obedience. As a missionary living with them, I followed their lifestyle. We trusted God to provide what we needed, and given our limited grocery budget, our first stop in each new city was at a local market to ask for donations for food.

I expected some bread past its best-before date or produce on the verge of rotting, so my eyeballs just about popped out of my head as I saw the shopping carts overflowing with all kinds of food items. Meats, cheeses, bread, and even fresh-cut flowers for the chapel. I was so struck by the unnecessary generosity of the Father. Realistically, all that was needed to survive was stale bread and water from the tap. But the flowers—I couldn't get past the flowers. This is why the bride in the original *Footwashing Series* image has an extravagant bunch of flowers sitting in her lap.

Do I have a poverty mindset toward the Lord—not the healthy kind that says, "I trust in God to provide," but one that says, "I expect just to scrape by with barely enough"?

What are the generous, unnecessary flowers the Father has laid in my lap?

In a way, there is an element of you within every person pictured sitting on the footwashing seat, as we are all part of His Bride. Somewhere over the last two thousand years we have lost sight of the value of footwashing—the way it is meant to be a consistent part of our lives—and I pray with equal elements of desperation and determination for the global Bride to wake up and start washing feet again. We are dishonoring and disobeying the Bridegroom when we ignore what He's asked us to do and how He's shown us to love each other.

ELEVEN

Anointing the Bridegroom

The Trigger

How wild to think that it was Mary's alabaster jar that triggered Judas to betray Jesus. The deciding factor wasn't one of the many "scandalous" teachings Jesus gave. It wasn't the way Jesus ruined funerals and raised the dead. It wasn't even His multiple declarations that He was God. It was Jesus receiving an expensive perfume anointing from a woman. Mary's radical worship was the defining moment that caused Judas to sell his leader and friend for a horribly small amount.

Does Jesus offend me?

> "Now when Jesus was at Bethany in the house of Simon the leper, a woman came up to him with an alabaster jar of very expensive ointment, and she poured it on his head, as he sat at table. But when the disciples saw it, they were indignant, saying, 'Why this waste? For this ointment might have been sold for a large sum, and given to the poor.' But Jesus, aware of this, said to them, 'Why do you trouble the woman? For she has done a beautiful thing to me. For you always have the poor with you, but you will not always have me. In pouring this ointment on my body she has done it to prepare me for burial. Truly, I say to you, wherever this gospel is preached in the whole world, what she has done will be told in memory of her.'

> "Then one of the twelve, who was called Judas Iscariot, went to the chief priests and said, 'What will you give me if I deliver him to you?' And they paid him thirty pieces of silver. And from that moment he sought an opportunity to betray him."
>
> Matthew 26:6–16

[Handwritten note: MARY'S WORSHIP WAS THE TRIGGER]

Forgiven Much, Loves Much

Theologians debate whether Mary with the alabaster jar is one and the same woman as Mary Magdalene, who was tormented with seven demons; traditionally they've been perceived as the same woman. Revealing the exact identity of Mary is not our focus in this chapter, but revealing what Mary's radical worship can still teach us today.

Jesus said the woman who poured her expensive perfume out on Him loved much because she'd been forgiven much (Luke 7:47). When I stay aware of how the Lord forgave my sins when I didn't deserve it, it bears fruit in several ways. I remain in a heart posture of thankfulness and adoration toward the Lord, and I must realize that the mercy I received from the Father is equally available for anyone else.

It would have been costly in more than just a financial way for Mary to pour that perfume on the feet of Jesus. There was the cost of her pride, the cost of making a scene in front of people, the cost of subjecting herself to ridicule and gossip.

Am I willing to sacrifice my pride in order to love Jesus in the way He deserves?

Anointing the Bridegroom

Mark 14:3 records that Mary's jar contained nard, a rare, precious ointment derived from the spikenard plant. Mary's jar was worth a year's wages, and modern commentators estimate that would be worth around US$50,000 today. No wonder there was an uproar when Mary poured the entire jar out onto someone's feet.

Because nard was expensive, it was often mixed with other oils of lesser value, or even counterfeited. The John 12 passage notes that the ointment Mary anointed Jesus' feet with was *pure* nard. There are no counterfeits or watered-down encounters with Jesus.

NOTHING WATERED DOWN WITH JESUS

> "Mary took a pound of costly ointment of pure nard and anointed the feet of Jesus and wiped his feet with her hair; and the house was filled with the fragrance of the ointment."
>
> John 12:3

Nard is mentioned twice outside of Mary anointing Jesus with it, both times in the Old Testament book of Song of Solomon.

> "While the king was on his couch,
>   My nard gave forth its fragrance."
>
> Song of Solomon 1:12

> "Your shoots are an orchard of pomegranates
>   with all choicest fruits,
>   henna with nard,
> nard and saffron, calamus and cinnamon,
>   with all trees of frankincense,
> myrrh and aloes,
>   with all chief spices—
> a garden fountain, a well of living water,
>   and flowing streams from Lebanon."
>
> Song of Solomon 4:13–15

The Song of Solomon can be interpreted through different lenses. One of the common interpretations of the book is that it is an illustration of the covenant love between God and His chosen people. This illustration would fit with one of the common uses of nard: to anoint a bride on the eve of her marriage. Perhaps Mary's action of anointing the Bridegroom was symbolically pointing toward our covenant relationship with God. Jesus' spilled-out blood was about to cover over the ways we had broken our covenant with Him.

Preparation for the Death of the Bridegroom

Nard was also one of the ointments used to prepare bodies for burial. Jesus even references this when he defends the actions of Mary:

> "Jesus said, 'Let her alone, let her keep it for the day of my burial. The poor you always have with you, but you do not always have me.'"
>
> John 12:7–8

Jesus knew His time was close. Mary's actions were prophetic, anointing Him for His death and burial.

Also, according to the Gospel of John, the Mary who poured out the jar of perfume was the sister of Lazarus. Lazarus had died and lain lifeless in a tomb for four days before Jesus came, wept, and then resurrected His friend. Perhaps the reason that Mary had access to such an expensive oil was because she had recently used it to anoint her own brother's body for burial.

If my sibling died and I'd used a particular perfume to prepare their dead body, I think I would have poured the entire rest of the bottle out on the feet of Jesus, the One who had raised them from the dead, too. I would thank Him with anything I had access to. I would empty the ointment associated with death onto Jesus' feet—the only One who had overcome it. That's a kind of God worth wasting $50,000 on the feet of.

Would I hesitate before offering Jesus something worth $50,000?

TWELVE

If You Can't Grab His Hands

Blood-Covered Feet

In Jewish law, a covenant was made by taking a calf, goat, ram, turtledove, and pigeon, and cutting the animals (except the birds) in half. Each half was placed opposite each other, and the two men making the covenant would walk through the middle of the halved animals (Genesis 15:9–10). It signified the seriousness of the agreement being made: "If I break this covenant, make me like the animals cut in two" (cf. Jeremiah 34:18–20). You can imagine the potentially bloody, messy feet after a covenant maker walked in between the separated animal pieces. It reminds me of the bloody feet of Jesus as He took the punishment *we* should have received for being the ones to break our covenant with Him. Jesus' own feet were pierced and nailed to a cross. The feet of God, bleeding as He upheld His covenant with us even when we had broken our side of the promise. Those are feet that I want to hold and worship.

Grab His Feet

I first heard this phrase as a ministry college classmate accepted a Mary of Bethany Award. The recipient of the award, Esther Gaspar, said that if you ever find yourself in a place where you can't grab His hands, to just grab His feet.

Some of us are in the process of building trust and relationship with God. It's difficult to maintain eye contact with someone who makes you nervous, whom you aren't completely comfortable around yet, or who intimidates you. Sometimes it's difficult to look God in the face.

Do I struggle to look God in the face? What am I afraid of seeing? Or am I afraid of being seen?

If you find it hard to look at God's face, you aren't alone. In the Old Testament, under the old covenant, Moses talked to God like a friend (Exodus 33:11), but God warned Moses that looking at His face and seeing His full glory would kill him (Exodus 33:18–23). God actually protected Moses by not revealing His face to him.

In the new covenant, we are given the ability to look at God (Jesus) in the face without fear. But there was still someone who avoided eye contact with Jesus.

> "And a great crowd followed him and thronged about him. And there was a woman who had had a flow of blood for twelve years, and who had suffered much under many physicians, and had spent all that she had, and was no better but rather grew worse. She had heard the reports about Jesus, and came up behind him in the crowd and touched his garment. For she said, 'If I touch even his garments, I shall be made well.' And immediately the hemorrhage ceased; and she felt in her body that she was healed of her disease. And Jesus, perceiving in himself that power had gone forth from him, immediately turned about in the crowd, and said, 'Who touched my garments?' And his disciples said to him, 'You see the crowd pressing around you, and yet you say, "Who touched me?"'
> And he looked around to see who had done it. But the woman, knowing what had been done to her, came in fear and trembling and fell down before him, and told him the whole truth. And he said to her, 'Daughter, your faith has made you well; go in peace, and be healed of your disease.'"
>
> Mark 5:24–34

[Handwritten annotations: "SHE DID ALL SHE COULD" pointing to "behind him in the crowd and touched his garment"; "AND IT WAS ENOUGH" pointing to "she was healed of her disease"; "HEALING IN SO MANY WAYS"]

This woman was considered ceremonially unclean under Jewish law due to her continual bleeding. Anyone and anything she touched would have also been considered temporarily unclean—as if her uncleanliness was contagious (Leviticus 15:25–27). Ongoing exclusion from religious and social activities for twelve painful years would have wounded her identity.

This woman of faith braved a massive crowd to get to Jesus; she plunged straight into the middle of the very people who had shunned and avoided her. She had not been permitted to enter the temple in twelve years due to being ritually unclean,[1] but I love that in this moment she made a beeline straight for Jesus, the spotless sacrifice. She didn't yell for Jesus or try to get His attention like so many others recorded in the Gospels. Instead, she wove through the crowd and, avoiding eye contact with Him, she quietly reached out and grasped the fringe of His garments.

If I saw Jesus in a crowd, what would I do? Yell? Run toward Him? Do nothing, and watch Him walk past me? Hide?

She didn't want to be seen by Jesus. She had been without physical contact or dignity for over a decade. Perhaps out of shame she avoided meeting His eyes and requesting her healing face to face. But her faith was enough to give her the courage to lean down low and touch the hem of His garment.

How did Jesus respond? Perhaps when He asked, "Who touched my garments?" she didn't immediately come forward because she was terrified of the possibility that she had made the Teacher ritually unclean. Or maybe she wondered if He would be angry that she reached out toward Him and His healing without asking permission first. But instead, perhaps more significant even than the physical healing she received, Jesus' first word to her restores her identity. "Daughter," He calls her in front of everyone.

There might be times when you feel as though in your relationship with the Lord, it's all you can do to reach out and grab His feet. Face first in the dirt, lying exhausted, all you have in you is to reach out and touch Him. Maybe you are afraid to meet His eyes; what if He is disappointed in you, angry with you, judges you? What if the fire in His eyes convicts you? What if you reach out toward Him, get His attention, and He doesn't know your name after all? Or maybe you feel like you don't

If You Can't Grab His Hands

want to disturb Him on His way to help other people whose needs are more important than your own.

The Lord will only ever respond to you with love. However you can reach for Him, reach out and grab ahold. If you're surrounded by crowds of people who judge you, do it anyway. Don't let anything hold you back from relationship with Him. He has so much healing to offer you, in many different ways. He will breathe one word as you make contact with Him: "Daughter."

If you can't grab His hands yet, grab His feet.

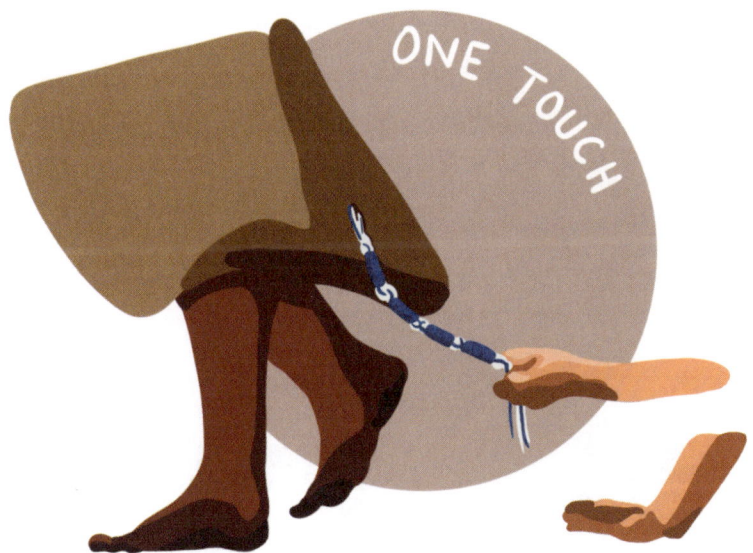

THIRTEEN

Interrupting Good Plans

Possibly the most popular image from *The Footwashing Series* artwork has been a matching set called "Anxiety and Peace." The "before" image shows a girl sitting curled up next to the footwashing stool, and Jesus opposite her, ready to wash her feet. Then the "after" image is the girl still curled up, but this time Jesus has moved and is sitting next to her on the ground with His arm around her.

The reason I drew it like this was because Jesus has always been willing to interrupt His "good" plans to meet us where we're at, in the way we need.

Interrupting the Good with the Needed

Think of Jesus in Mark 5 on His way to Jairus's house to save a dying twelve-year-old daughter. But along the way He stopped to encounter the woman who had been bleeding for twelve years. (The parallels in these two simultaneous stories are incredible.)

If I were Jesus, I probably would have assessed the situation a little differently. I wouldn't have stopped to help a woman who had already waited twelve years for a healing moment—after all, another day or even a few hours wouldn't have changed much when she'd made it through twelve years already—not when every second counted for a little girl dying. But Jesus was willing to interrupt His good plans (hurrying to Jairus's house to save a girl's life) in order to encounter someone and restore a woman's life.

One of the many aspects of the Last Supper foot-washing that stands out to me is the fact that Jesus interrupted a good thing (a final meal with His closest friends, knowing He was going to die the next day) to encounter them in the way they needed: washing their feet.

NOT AFTER— DURING

"And during supper Jesus, knowing that the Father had given all things into his hands, and that he had come from God and was going to God, got up from the table, took off his outer robe, and tied a towel around himself. ...

"After he had washed their feet, had put on his robe, and had returned to the table, he said to them, 'Do you know what I have done to you?'"

John 13:2–4, 12 NRSVA

I'M WORTH INTERRUPTING A GOOD THING FOR

Jesus is always ready to meet us and minister to us in the way we need. He's not afraid of good plans—ours or someone else's—being interrupted in order to encounter us.

Sometimes we feel that God has better things to do, more important things, more important people to tend to than our own needs. It can look like not wanting to bother Jesus by asking Him to heal your headache when someone else has cancer. It can look like not asking God for His opinion on a decision you have to make because you doubt He'd be interested in which car you buy or job offer you accept. It's a quiet belief masquerading as selflessness that God isn't interested in talking with you or helping you because others have greater needs.

Do I think the needs of others are more important than my own? Do I believe that God isn't interested in me unless I'm in crisis?

A person who primarily encounters God when there is a crisis may subconsciously pursue a state of constant crisis because that's where they meet God most strongly. There's always a spiritual battle, always a family crisis, always a health struggle, always an attack from the Enemy. But if you're in constant communion with God, believing that He's equally as interested in your everyday life as in your moments of hardship, there's no need to create a sense of crisis in order to see (or prove) His presence in your life. He's always present, always interested, and He will always stop and see you in a crowd.

If mental health is causing you to seek God in a crowd, you're worth interrupting His plans for.

If heartbreak is why you're reaching for the hem of His cloak, He will stop for you.

If doubt is the reason you're hiding your eyes, Jesus calls you "Daughter."

If chronic disease is what you're grabbing on to His garment for, He is proud of your faith.

If infertility is why you're braving a crowd, Jesus sees you among them all.

If addiction is why you need a touch from Jesus, let His power fill you.

If we're too much of a mess to get ourselves onto the footwashing seat, or we're reaching out in a crowd hoping for the "one touch" that can change everything, Jesus will interrupt His good plans and meet us exactly as and where we are. He's the kind of God to get up from where He was kneeling, ready to wash our feet, and come and put an arm around us while we sit, messy and exhausted, on the floor.

FOURTEEN

Healing Trauma

Washing Feet in the Middle East

The Uber dropped off the outreach team I was leading at the entrance to a dark back alley in the Middle East at nine o'clock one evening, and I wondered uneasily whether this was a bit *too* out there, in the scheme of risky things I'd done for Jesus. We didn't even have a proper address, just a virtual pin on a map indicating where to find a woman we'd been asked to minister to.

We climbed several flights of stairs in what felt like an unfinished concrete apartment building. There were no railings, and gaping holes peeked into the dark night sky where windowpanes should have been. A sweet, petite woman answered the door and ushered us inside her apartment. She wept as she shared through a translator about the pain she'd endured, and she was transformed as she radically forgave. A grandfather from our small team knelt on the floor in front of her and washed her feet. There wasn't a dry eye in the room as he quietly apologized for the way she had been treated and tenderly washed her feet in a dirty white bucket.

We walked out of that tall concrete building at midnight, exhausted and utterly undone by how God had moved. I knew footwashing would hold a different meaning to me from that night onward. I had drawn images of imaginary people having their feet washed, but this was someone real. This was an actual life. I saw the difference an encounter with Jesus through footwashing could make. It wasn't the water that was changing her life—it was the God she was meeting through it.

Trauma

Like the woman in the Middle East, I wish we weren't as familiar with trauma as we are, but it's the reason I want to talk about this. Because for so many people, it's real life. And I need us to know that footwashing is applicable for real life. That footwashing is made for the hardest moments of life, like living through pain. That this is where Jesus meets us. Where we need Him most.

> I'm sorry if trauma is your story.
> I'm sorry if it came from someone who should have protected you.
> I'm sorry if you were young.
> I'm sorry if you were any age.
> I'm sorry if it was perpetrated by a church leader who should have been safe.
> I'm sorry if it came from someone you trusted.
> I'm sorry if it was caused by someone you loved.
> I'm sorry if it came from a stranger.
> I'm sorry if your body was hurt.
> I'm sorry if things could have been done.
> I'm sorry if your emotions were twisted around.
> I'm sorry if your fire was dampened.
> I'm sorry if your spirit was crushed.
> I'm sorry if you were made to feel as though your mind wasn't trustworthy.
> I'm sorry if you couldn't breathe.
> I'm sorry if you thought you deserved it.
> I'm sorry if they told you that you imagined it.
> I'm sorry if it felt like the life was sucked out of your future for a minute.
> I'm sorry if you felt like you couldn't tell anyone.
> I'm sorry if you told someone and they didn't do anything, or blamed you, or made it worse.

If you resonate with any of this . . . I'm sorry. I'm praying you feel Him close if panic rises. Feel Jesus holding your hand.

Do I have any areas of trauma I need Jesus to heal? Do I trust Him with them?

The Jesus You Need

Trauma and areas of pain are often where we want to run away from Jesus because we feel so exposed, vulnerable, and unsure of who to trust. Our priority is self-protection, making sure no one else can touch or exploit the most tender, ruined parts of ourselves.

I want to introduce you to Someone who is the most trustworthy person to let into this area. The kind of Person who would let himself be stripped naked so that you could have His robe while He was exposed.

Jesus knows what it's like. He was abused too. He endured it all, from the humiliation and the judgment to the beating and the blood, so if you had to go through something like that you aren't alone. There is Someone who understands, even if it feels like you're the only one.

When I drew these "Abuse + Healing" pictures within *The Footwashing Series*, it felt risky—sacrilegious?—drawing Jesus without His clothes. Massively undignified. But I know two things about Jesus.

This is what He did.

And this is what He would do.

He was stripped of His robe so that we could be clothed in everything good His agony bought us. And when He sees us at our most vulnerable, He tenderly offers His robe.

> "But he was wounded for our transgressions,
>   he was bruised for our iniquities;
> upon him was the chastisement that made us whole,
>   and with his stripes we are healed."
>
> Isaiah 53:5

HIS WOUNDS MADE A WAY
FOR MINE TO BE HEALED

Whatever you've been through, whether it was mental, physical, spiritual or emotional, there's healing on offer from Jesus for you. Nothing is too impossible to redeem or heal. Have a look in the Scriptures; if Jesus can open blind eyes, set people free, and raise the dead, He can for sure heal you too.

I know there's a lot that goes into a healing process, and I would encourage you to seek support from trusted friends and professional people. I'm just trying to remind you not to cut Jesus out of the equation. Therapy will give you skills to cope, medicine can assist, and a psychologist can help identify what you're experiencing, but God is the one who can do a long-term, permanent healing in you.

> "But now thus says the LORD,
>   he who created you, O Jacob,
>   he who formed you, O Israel:
> 'Fear not, for I have redeemed you;
>   I have called you by name, you are mine.
> When you pass through the waters I will be with you;
>   and through the rivers, they shall not overwhelm you;
> when you walk through fire you shall not be burned,
>   and the flame shall not consume you.'"
>
> Isaiah 43:1–2

*IMPOSSIBLE TO SURVIVE...
BUT, JESUS.*

You might feel as though you've been drowning, or as though a wildfire has ravaged your future and burned you so badly you don't know if you can survive, but Jesus has been with you the whole time, and He won't leave you now. He can redeem anything. He sees your pain, recognizes your brokenness, and calls you by your real name. Not "Broken," "Hopeless," or "Unfixable" but "Precious," "Honored," "Redeemed," and "Loved."

> "Because you are precious in my eyes,
>   And honored, and I love you."
>
> Isaiah 43:4

Jesus is holding out His robe to you, friend. You can trust Him. He knows pain. And He's the safest man in the universe.

Jesus is holding out His robe to me—will I take it?

Whatever you've been through, He is ready when you are to gently wash your feet, restore you, heal you, clothe you, redeem it all. He is the safest place. If the Jesus you met or people told you about wasn't this radically loving, maybe it wasn't the real Jesus. But this one . . . He's waiting with His robe for you.

FIFTEEN

Your Worship Is Never a Waste

My Alabaster Jar

When I think of Mary pouring out her perfume and ministering to the feet of Jesus, I think of the different ways we can "waste" our love on Him. Ways that might look unreasonable to anyone else, but that He receives as a priceless offering.

Worship can be so many different things. Our personal alabaster jar of worship might be

- Praising Him when we're in pain
- Faithfulness to God when we haven't seen the miracle we've been praying for
- Holding on to a promise when it's taking longer than expected
- Giving away finances when it doesn't make sense
- Spending longer in prayer when there are so many things fighting for our attention
- Quitting a job that gives security to follow Him down a different avenue
- Breaking up with the person God is prompting us to
- Moving to another country
- Getting up in the night for our children

What is my alabaster jar of worship I have to offer the Lord in my current season?

One of the things I love about this image of Mary breaking open a jar is that the lid isn't just taken off. There are no take-backs with breaking open the jar. The perfume that spilled out can't be put back inside.

"She broke the jar and poured it over his head."

Mark 14:3

Another thing I love is that in wiping His feet with the perfume and our hair, we come out smelling just as sweet and powerfully as Jesus. Covered in the fragrance of worship. Worship of God affects us on a personal level.

"Mary took a pound of costly ointment of pure nard and anointed the feet of Jesus and wiped his feet with her hair..."

John 12:3a

MARY CAME AWAY SMELLING OF PERFUME TOO.

PROXIMITY TO JESUS = HOW MUCH I "SMELL" LIKE HIM

Worship also affects those around us on a corporate level. Worship overflows onto others and affects an environment. When Mary anointed the feet of Jesus, the whole house was filled with the fragrance of her worship. Even those who criticized the worship received the gift of its fragrance.

"... and the house was filled with the fragrance of the ointment."

John 12:3b

We can learn from Mary about the way we can show our love for Jesus: pour our offering out on His feet. Jesus washes our feet; we anoint His.

Is There Any Kind of Offering God Is Not Worthy Of?

I have had the heartbreaking privilege of praying multiple times for a miracle resurrection alongside parents who had unexpectedly lost their child. Joining them as they declared that God was still good and worthy of worship no matter the outcome left a deep mark on me. The sweet children remained safe in the arms of Jesus in heaven, and there are many who would have seen that as evidence of worship being a waste. A waste of time, a waste of emotional energy, a waste of faith. But our circumstances shouldn't determine whether or not God is worthy of our praise. When I am convinced that the intrinsic and only nature of God is that He is good, I understand that He is always worth my worship, even on the worst day of my life. Worship is never a waste.

Ornate Cathedrals

We recognize the presence of God, but sometimes we can still balk at the costly worship that other people can offer Him. Like Judas, we may look at ornate cathedrals (for example) and say, "We could have given the money to the poor instead!"

It is not that supporting the struggling and marginalized in our communities is not important. That is a vital part of our God-given mission. But it always comes back to our hearts. The Gospel of John records that Judas only protested and said the perfume could have been sold and the money used for the poor because he was a thief and was stealing from the ministry savings (John 12:4–6).

Judas sold Jesus—the One who made him, loved him, and continued to offer him forgiveness and redemption—for thirty silver coins. It's estimated that the monetary value of those silver coins was the equivalent of approximately US$90–$3,000 today. Not even an unthinkable, irresistible amount for most people. A pitiful amount to betray God for—although how could there ever be an appropriate financial price put on God?

Compare the amount Judas sold Jesus for ($90–$3,000) to the amount Mary worshiped Him with ($50,000). The values tell a story of their own.

My Silver Coins

It's easy to judge the actions of Judas, but what are we willing to deny Jesus or sell Him out for? What are we prioritizing above the Lord?

What would my thirty silver coins be?

The ultimate question is, What do we think God is worth? Are golden cathedrals too extravagant? Is becoming a missionary too radical? Is crying in Walmart over the posters of missing children too ridiculous?

Do I ever struggle with judging the ways others pour out their love for Jesus? What does Jesus think of their way of loving Him?

I want to be someone who says, "There's no worship that's too extravagant." If it's a laid-down life He's looking for, He can have mine. He's worthy. Worship is never a waste.

Whatever I have to give Him, He's worth it.

SIXTEEN

Keeping Your Heart Soft

The Offering of a Soft Heart

As I stood in the checkout line in Walmart, a line of posters advertising missing children caught my eye. My friend and I pushed our shopping cart over, and I stood and looked at the faces of all the missing children, read their names and ages, and prayed for them to be found. I literally couldn't stop the tears from rolling down my cheeks. My heart ached as I looked at the photographs and wondered what had happened to them and who was searching for them.

I like having a soft heart. For the longest time, as a defense mechanism against pain, I intentionally hardened my heart so I couldn't be hurt. Shutting down my emotions protected me against painful feelings, but it also meant my experience of God's heart—and my own!—was limited.
It takes courage to allow God to give us new hearts as He spoke about in Ezekiel:

TAKES COURAGE

> "A new heart I will give you, and a new spirit I will put within you; and I will take out of your flesh the heart of stone and give you a heart of flesh."
>
> Ezekiel 36:26

TAKES VULNERABILITY

I prioritized the Lord healing my heart and waking it up again because first, I wanted to be the healthiest version of myself that God designed me

to be! And second, I wanted to be sensitive to the Holy Spirit. I want to see with His eyes, hear with His ears, think with His mind, and feel with His heart. When I shut down my heart, I also shut down my ability to feel His heart for people, places, and situations.

Compassion

Feeling His heart is a way we can have insight into what's on His mind and how we can partner with His good plans. For example, when I felt His heart for the missing children on the notice board in Walmart, feeling the grief that they were missing led to me praying for them to be returned safely home. When I shut off my heart, I shut off the ability to be moved by the Lord's compassion toward people and to pray and act in accordance with what God wants to do in the lives of those He loves.

Unfortunately, often we are under the impression that experiencing emotion is a weakness. Men are told to "man up" and raised with the mantra "Boys don't cry." There is pressure for women to leave emotions outside of the workplace or believe they are unsuitable for leadership because of the softness of their hearts. We're missing something incredibly vital; God created us with emotions. *God* has emotions! Jesus got angry, Jesus cried when His friend died, Jesus was moved with compassion, and amidst all of that—Jesus was the healthiest man on the planet.

The Gospels specifically remark that Jesus was moved by *compassion* to heal people (Matthew 14:14), multiply food (Matthew 15:32–38), teach the lost (Mark 6:34), and raise the dead (Luke 7:11–15).

> "And when Jesus went out He saw a great multitude; and He was moved with compassion for them, and healed their sick."
>
> Matthew 14:14 NKJV

If Jesus operated out of compassion by having a heart that could fully feel, so should I.

Have I shut down my heart?

What do I believe about emotions? What was I taught about them?

Jesus also specifically highlighted compassion as the motivating factor in multiple parables He told.

The Prodigal Son

> "And he arose and came to his father. But while he was yet at a distance, his father saw him and had compassion, and ran and embraced him and kissed him."
>
> Luke 15:20

COMPASSION WAS A CATALYST FOR FORGIVENESS + LED TO RESTORED RELATIONSHIP

→ COMPASSION RESTORES US TO THE FATHER

The Good Samaritan

> "Jesus replied, 'A man was going down from Jerusalem to Jericho, and he fell among robbers, who stripped him and beat him, and departed, leaving him half dead. Now by chance a priest was going down that road; and when he saw him he passed by on the other side. So likewise a Levite, when he came to the place and saw him, passed by on the other side. But a Samaritan, as he journeyed, came to where he was; and when he saw him, he had compassion, and went to him and bound up his wounds, pouring on oil and wine; then he set him on his own beast and brought him to an inn, and took care of him.'"
>
> Luke 10:30–34

COMPASSION SAVED A LIFE

Compassion is what caused a man to stop and help his enemy, and it's a lack of compassion that caused two others to pass by a man on the brink of death.

Feeling His heart and having the ability to be moved by compassion helps us love individuals in the way that God intends us to. Keep your heart soft. It will allow you to experience the fullness of your emotions and to be moved by the compassion you feel to respond to others in the way Jesus would. Compassion will prompt you to pick up a towel and wash feet.

SEVENTEEN

Love Is a Decision

Toward the end of the Gospel of John, one of the key themes Jesus repeats over and over is to "love one another." After Jesus washed the feet of the disciples, he said to them,

INSTRUCTION

> "A new command I give you: Love one another. As I have loved you, so you must love one another. By this everyone will know that you are my disciples, if you love one another."
>
> John 13:34–35 NIV

Love

A commandment is not a suggestion. Jesus is not saying, "Love each other if you feel like it." It is an order to follow from our Messiah. Under the old covenant Law, there were 613 commandments which had to be meticulously followed. Jesus gave us a new command over and over—to love each other. He doesn't just say it once—He repeats the same words again:

> "This is my commandment, that you love one another as I have loved you."
>
> John 15:12

Sometimes it feels easy and natural to love people. The feeling in my heart matches up with Jesus' order for my actions. My experience of

someone when they've acted with love toward me makes it easy to respond with love toward them in return. But there are some people who really challenge me. The quickest way to infuriate me is to lie to me because I have such a high value for integrity. In moments like those, when I am fuming with anger, it is not about whether someone *deserves* a response of love, but whether I have such a revelation of the love of Jesus in my own life that I must respond with love . . . regardless of the behavior of someone else.

What is my reputation for how I treat people? How do I treat people I struggle with?

"If any one says, 'I love God,' and hates his brother, he is a liar; for he who does not love his brother whom he has seen, cannot love God whom he has not seen. And this commandment we have from him, that he who loves God should love his brother also."

1 John 4:20–21

Fruit of the Spirit

This verse challenges me to take a good hard look at the reality of my love. Love is the first fruit of the Spirit, which means it can be grown. I can grow my ability to love people just as much as I can grow my self-control muscle in my life, or any other fruit of the Spirit.

"But the fruit of the Spirit is love, joy, peace, patience, kindness, goodness, faithfulness, gentleness, self-control; against such there is no law."

Galatians 5:22–23

Which of these fruits are healthy in my life, and which are small or nonexistent currently? How can I water them?

Which of these primarily ring true for me?

How I Respond to People

How I Respond to People	What My Response Reveals About Me
I treat people with honor and love *only* when they deserve it.	Love is not a decision I'm making; it's a conditional reaction depending on how someone treats *me*.
I treat everyone with love *regardless* of whether they treat me with honor or dishonor.	Love is an intentional decision and hallmark of my character. I have a personal revelation of God's love toward me.

If responding with love toward people is challenging for you, here are some hints for how to develop love for others in your life and keep washing their feet when, really, you want to douse them in water instead.

1. **Ask God how He sees that person.** What does He think of them? What encouraging names does He call them by? What is His good plan for their life? What does He love about them? What gifts do they carry?
2. **Dwell on the intrinsic value that each person on the planet has** as someone whom God made, whom God loves, who is irreplaceable, and who is worth dying for.

    > "For you created my inmost being;
    >   you knit me together in my mother's womb.
    > I praise you because I am fearfully and wonderfully made;
    >   your works are wonderful,
    >   I know that full well."
    >
    > Psalm 139:13–14 NIV

3. **Ask God for forgiveness** for the times you have not responded with love to people. After you confess your sin to Him, remember His mercy covers you.

    > "The LORD is merciful and gracious,
    >   slow to anger and abounding in steadfast love.
    > He will not always chide,
    >   nor will he keep his anger for ever.

> He does not deal with us according to our sins,
> 	nor requite us according to our iniquities.
> For as the heavens are high above the earth,
> 	so great is his steadfast love toward those who fear him;
> as far as the east is from the west,
> 	so far does he remove our transgressions from us."
>
> Psalm 103:8–12

4. **Reflect back on your own life before Jesus saved you.** What was it like, or would it have been like, without Jesus stepping in and rescuing you? What did His death on the cross purchase for you? What have you been forgiven for?

   Do you remember what Jesus said about Mary, who poured out her perfume on His feet? That she who is forgiven much loves much. And we have been forgiven much.

   > "Therefore I tell you, her sins, which are many, are forgiven, for she loved much; but he who is forgiven little, loves little."
   >
   > Luke 7:47

LOVE IS NOT A FEELING

EIGHTEEN

True Love and Free Will

"Footwashing isn't saying they were all saved and went to heaven. In my opinion, it's saying that Jesus is willing to clean the places where you've walked. 'I'm [Jesus] here to cleanse you from the places you've walked. You have to decide if you're going to walk back there again, right? You have to decide—after I get you all cleaned up—are you going to go back to the pig farm? Well okay, I'll be here to wash them again.'"[1]

Kris Vallotton

We have to talk about the concept that Jesus would only wash the feet of those who were already following Him, had accepted Him as Lord and Savior, and got up from the chair and lived a perfect life following Jesus. All three of these presumptions are biblically incorrect given that Jesus washed the feet of very flawed disciples—one of whom permanently walked away from Him.

Free Will

It is crucial to our relationship with God that He created us with free will. We are not robots or puppets programmed to worship Him without any choice of whether we want relationship with Him. He created us in His image, *imago Dei*, in all ways, including our ability to express and receive genuine love as a result of free will.

Right from the beginning God created Adam and Eve with free will. God didn't create the tree of the knowledge of good and evil and hide it in the very back corner of the Garden. He didn't hide its existence from the humans He created and loved. He put the tree in plain sight and told them about it (Genesis 2:9, 15–17).

We used our free will to turn our backs on God and create separation between us and our Maker, and throughout history we've continued to use it to draw us closer to the Lord and also to cause further betrayal and separation.

How have I used my free will? To walk closer toward God, or away from Him?

When the angel appeared to Mary, she had a freewill choice in front of her: Would she partner with God's plans or walk away from what was clearly going to be a difficult path? With her *yes* to God, she untied the knot of Eve's *no* to Him.

> "And Mary said, 'Behold, I am the handmaid of the Lord; let it be to me according to your word.' And the angel departed from her."
>
> Luke 1:38

"MARY'S FIAT"

"FIAT MIHI SECUNDUM VERBUM TUUM"
LATIN FOR "LET IT BE DONE TO ME ACCORDING TO YOUR WORD."

True Love

It's free will that makes real love possible. Without free will—the ability to choose to love someone or not—all we're left with is a warped version of love that reeks of control, manipulation, and use. It's the kind of love that says things like

> "Give me what I want from you, or I'll leave you."
> "I want part of you, but not all of you."
> "I won't commit to you in marriage because this way I have a sense of control over you through the constant threat of leaving."
> "If you leave this relationship, I'll expose you."
> "I won't give you too much of myself in case it's not returned."
> "I'll only love you if you meet these conditions."

Can you imagine the Lord ever threatening to leave you if you didn't give Him what He wanted? His love was and is the opposite of this. No matter how many times we break our covenant with Him, He continues to faithfully love us.

True, real love says things like

"I see you, I know you, I love you, and I still choose you."
"I want all of you."
"I'm risking my heart for the possibility of relationship with you."
"You get to choose whether you want to commit to me too."
"I don't want there to be fear in our relationship."
"I will sacrifice for your good."

What has my experience of love been? Have I tried to control anyone out of fear? Am I giving and receiving real love in my relationships, or are there undertones of manipulation?

Free Will Today

Nothing has changed. We still have every opportunity to walk toward God or walk away from Him. When it comes to the footwashing stool, just as in the Garden, God gives us total freedom to sit down on it or not. And He won't control how we behave after we get up from it.

The pigpen that Kris Vallotton referred to during our discussion about footwashing on his podcast is referencing the Prodigal Son. When the son returned home, the father met him with open arms and clothed him in appropriate attire for a son again. But the father had no guarantee that the son would stay and live out his reclaimed identity and forgiveness. The son could have left his father and responsibilities and made a mess of his life again—returned to the pigpen—if he chose to.

When we, or anyone, sit down on the footwashing stool for Jesus to wash us clean from the mess of our past, He does so with no guarantee of what our response will be. Will I get up, clothed in the best robe, ring on my finger, shoes on my feet, stomach full of the feast the Father prepared for me, and walk down the same dusty road to the pigpen again? He will let me. He honors my free will, and that's what makes the love that I offer Him real.

NINETEEN

Performance

Judas Heard It All

Judas heard all His sermons
Judas saw all the miracles
Judas prayed and saw people healed through his very own hands
But hadn't given Jesus his heart.
You can go to church
Read the Bible
Sing the worship songs
Have your feet washed
Operate in the spiritual gifts
Preach the house down
Respond to the altar call
Tell Him you're loyal
Kiss His cheek
And still not give him your heart.

Performance and the Heart

Performance without intimacy will create resentment.

In Luke 18, Jesus tells the parable of a Pharisee and a tax collector. In the story, the two men both performed the same action—praying to God at the temple. But Jesus said only one of the men was justified through prayer. Why?

Performance

> [COMPARISON ROBBED HIM OF RELATIONSHIP WITH GOD]
>
> "Two men went up into the temple to pray, one a Pharisee and the other a tax collector. The Pharisee stood and prayed thus with himself, 'God, I thank thee that I am not like other men, extortioners, unjust, adulterers, or even like this tax collector. I fast twice a week, I give tithes of all that I get.' But the tax collector, standing far off, would not even lift up his eyes to heaven, but beat his breast, saying, 'God, be merciful to me a sinner!' I tell you, this man went down to his house justified rather than the other; for every one who exalts himself will be humbled, but he who humbles himself will be exalted."
>
> Luke 18:10–14

[WAS HONEST WITH GOD — SAW HIS NEED FOR GOD]

The tax collector and the Pharisee both performed the same action—prayer. But the heart posture behind the prayer was what mattered to the Lord. The Pharisee made the right action in the legal sense—he had done all the right things. But it was the tax collector who came before the Lord with a heart of humility in his prayer.

The prophet Hosea wrote from God's heart: "For I desire mercy, not sacrifice, and acknowledgment of God rather than burnt offerings" (Hosea 6:6 NIV), and Jesus repeated the passage to the Pharisees (Matthew 12:7). It was clear that the right actions, even fulfilling the Law perfectly, were no longer enough. God wanted more. God wanted the *heart* behind the action.

During the famous Matthew 5 Sermon on the Mount, Jesus makes it clear that while the old covenant was about actions, the new covenant is about heart posture. Under the old covenant, it was sufficient to technically keep your marriage covenant vows through your actions. But Jesus introduces a new standard, one where even the heart matters.

> "You have heard that it was said, 'You shall not commit adultery.' But I say to you that every one who looks at a woman lustfully has already committed adultery with her in his heart."
>
> Matthew 5:27–28

Judas's Performance Was Perfect

Because none of the disciples suspected that Judas was the betrayer in their midst, we can conclude that Judas's actions were perfect to the outward eye. None of the other eleven men who lived and ministered in close proximity with Judas thought it possible that he was the betrayer, even as it unfolded in front of their eyes. Judas must have spoken, acted, and performed miracles like a true disciple. His actions must have made it appear that he truly loved Jesus. There was no indication that he didn't belong with the followers of Jesus. He had all of the action . . . and none of the heart. Mary's alabaster jar poured out was simply the catalyst in ending the disconnect between his actions and his heart posture.

Performance can look many different ways in our life today. It can look like attending church because it's a part of your culture or what your family expects. It can look like praying not out of love, but out of a fear of being judged. It can look like being a Christian in public, but in private struggling with sexual sin and leading a double life.

Am I "performing" in any area of my life? Is there a disconnect between my heart and actions? Am I only doing "religious things" to avoid punishment or judgment?

Performance is exhausting.

There's only so long that you can play a part before cracks are revealed, mistakes are made, and bitterness sets in.

Performance

A heart that is performing actions without authentic love will lead to intimacy without commitment.

SO PAINFUL

> "His betrayer had given them a sign: 'The One I kiss, He's the One; arrest Him!' So he went right up to Jesus and said, 'Greetings, Rabbi!' and kissed Him. 'Friend,' Jesus asked him, 'why have you come?'"
>
> Matthew 26:48–50 HCSB

HE GIVES US SO MANY CHANCES TO RETURN TO HIM WITHOUT FEAR

Judas's betrayal sign of a greeting kiss on the cheek was an illustration of intimacy without commitment.

Jesus, help me to match my level of commitment to my level of intimacy with You. I never want to kiss your cheek and betray you at the same time.

Performance vs. Discipline

So what about moments when you don't feel like apologizing or forgiving? What about going to church or singing in worship when you don't feel it? Is it performance—empty actions without a correct heart posture? We already talked about love being a choice not a feeling. Is washing feet inauthentic if we choose to do it but don't have a feeling in our heart of *wanting* to do it?

There are times when we aren't going to feel the heart behind our actions. This doesn't make them disingenuous; it can be a form of discipline. It can be using our actions and mind to tell our heart to get in line.

Empty actions are usually motivated by a desire to be approved of by others, a fear of being found out, or a need to earn approval from God. This is different from choosing to do what is right and good, even when you don't *feel* the motivation to do it. I don't feel like opening my Bible each day, but I do it because I know that it's good for me, regardless of whether I feel like it at the time. I don't feel like forgiving someone after they've wounded me and are apologizing, but I choose to do it because I know unforgiveness and bitterness will make me sick and go against what Jesus asked me to do.

There will be times when you don't feel like washing feet. Times when you would rather yell in frustration than extend grace. Times when someone has turned back to addiction and now wants to sit down on the seat again, and you really don't have the patience to meet them with the same loving response for the fifth time.

You can still choose to wash feet, even if you don't feel like it. Who knows, maybe there was a hesitation or grief in Jesus' heart that He chose to overcome when He washed the disciples' feet too.

TWENTY

Repetitive Failure

Seventeen-year-old Jessica was left reeling after the earthquakes. To give a fuller picture, Christchurch, New Zealand, didn't just endure one earthquake—we had a sequence of four huge earthquakes and over 11,200 aftershocks over the space of sixteen months after the first significant earthquake.[1] That works out to be an earthquake or aftershock approximately once an hour, all throughout the day and night, for over a year. It was exhausting and left no space to heal, as each unexpected violent jolt and rumble brought all the trauma of surviving the main earthquake straight back to the surface. Every time the earth shook, I remembered the cars sinking into holes in the ground, the man running past yelling for help rescuing people in a partially collapsed hotel, the beefy colleague who rode a motorcycle to work each day bent over vomiting from shock, the people lying bleeding in the hospital car park.

The Question That's More Important Than "Is God Real?"

The earthquake forced me to wrestle with the one question everyone has to ask at some point in their life, and it's one that is perhaps even more important than "Is God real?" That question is, "Is God good?" There are people who acknowledge that God is real but still reject relationship with Him over the way they answer that question. If you think that God is mean, or doesn't care about you, or is manipulative, or makes bad things happen

to you—that's not a God you would want relationship with! But if you believe God can *only* be good, even in the middle of something awful or unforgivable, that will change Him from being the person that you want to run away from to being the person that you want to run to.

Do I believe God is real?

Do I believe God is good?

Peter and Judas

If we go back to Peter and Judas, I propose that the way they either ran from Jesus or toward Him after they each betrayed Him reveals how they would have answered the question, "Is God good?" Whether we run toward God or away from Him in our pain and shame tells us what kind of Father we think He is. I wonder if Judas's life could have had a different outcome if he believed that God would have met him with kindness and forgiveness in his failure? In Luke 15, even after the Prodigal Son had squandered and wasted his portion of his father's inheritance, the moment he decided to return home was when he remembered his father's nature, that he was good.

Repetitive Failure

One of the things that can keep us away from the footwashing seat is embarrassment and shame that we've messed up again. No one wants to walk up to Jesus and say, "Hey Jesus, it's me again. Back with the same sin. Back to ask forgiveness for the exact same thing you forgave me for last time and I promised I wouldn't do again." The shame and disappointment of failure can keep us from running straight toward Jesus when we mess up. Not to mention how disheartening and exhausting it can feel to battle out an addiction or repetitive sin. The loss of hope to ever be truly free can make it difficult to find motivation to approach the throne again and ask for forgiveness when a sinking voice in the back of your mind whispers it is pointless since you will mess up again anyway.

> *Do I struggle with the same sin over and over? Do I still ask God's forgiveness every time I sin in this area? Do I have hope that I can overcome this and have permanent, lasting freedom?*

If we are convinced that we will only be met by love when we return to God—no matter whether it's the first time or the thousandth time that we're running into His arms—our instinct will continue to be to run toward Him when we've messed up instead of running away from Him in shame or fear. God doesn't have a limit to His mercy or His patience with us. He is "gracious and merciful, slow to anger and abounding in steadfast love" (Psalm 145:8). He is the one who told *us* to forgive without limits.

> "Then Peter came up and said to him, 'Lord, how often shall my brother sin against me, and I forgive him? As many as seven times?' Jesus said to him, 'I do not say to you seven times, but seventy times seven.'"
>
> Matthew 18:21–22

[Handwritten note: NOT A LITERAL NUMBER—REPRESENTS LIMITLESS FORGIVENESS]

Who do I expect to meet when I return to God after I mess up—an angry Father or a kind one?

The footwashing stool doesn't have a limited number of times you can sit down on it. It doesn't have an expiration date. It isn't a one-time offer, and it doesn't get locked away once you've used it a certain number of times. It is available—HE is available—as many times as we want and need to sit down. The same compassionate Jesus is there whether we're sitting down for an encounter because we're exhausted or to confess that we've watched pornography for the four hundredth time. His response to us won't ever change.

Friends

With your own feet still damp from where Jesus washed them, it's time to do what He asked: Pick up a towel, fill a basin with fresh water, get low, and wash feet. Footwashing, whether literal or metaphorical, can change a life . . . or even a legacy. What if you change history by the way you kneel to wash feet? Get ready for some countercultural ideas in the "Friends" section.

TWENTY-ONE

Love Looks Like Something

The Goat

One of my first times attending Sunday school at church, the children were fundraising together for a goat for a family in Africa. I can't say I knew who Jesus was, but even as an eleven-year-old my heart was moved by kids giving their pocket money for a goat to help a family they didn't know on the other side of the world. The goat was strangely instrumental in my decision to say yes to giving my life to Jesus not long after. Seeing the physical act of compassion in followers of Jesus helped convince me of the reality of God.

Our love of God, following Him, must manifest as something tangible.

> "So faith by itself, if it has no works, is dead."
> James 2:17

This doesn't mean that good behavior or actions can earn salvation or the love of God. It means that when we are met by the love of God in our own lives, it must come out looking like something tangible. It manifests in the ways we treat people, talk to people, serve people. Jesus didn't just tell a story

about washing feet, He really knelt and did it. It's not enough for us to talk about washing feet—we need to turn our words and beliefs into real actions in times when it's called for.

Saint Teresa of Calcutta

I didn't realize that Mother Teresa's ministry was so radical until I was in India myself and had a firsthand experience of a primarily Hindu nation. Mother Teresa is famous for founding the Missionaries of Charity, a religious order dedicated to helping the poor in the slums of India.

One of the reasons Mother Teresa's work was so controversial was that it disrupted a deeply ingrained belief system. India is a heavily Hindu nation, and some devout Hindus see suffering as a consequence of karma.

Karma says you get what you deserve.

Christianity says Jesus took the punishment you deserved and freely gave what you could never earn.

Many believed Mother Teresa's actions were culturally inappropriate as she intervened to care for people from lower castes in India, including the untouchable caste (Dalits), who were often neglected or left to die on the streets. Some devout Hindus felt that by alleviating the suffering of the poor, she was robbing them of their chance to earn a better position in the next life through karma. Mother Teresa faced numerous challenges in order to be the hands and feet of Jesus and wash feet (spiritually as well as literally), including exposure to serious diseases, resistance from some Hindu extremists, protests against her work, harassment, threats, bureaucratic resistance, and personal risk while caring for the injured and abandoned during the 1970s Calcutta Riots.

She touched the untouchables—and doesn't that sound like something Jesus did?

Who are the "untouchables" in my life I can serve?

The Good Samaritan

The Good Samaritan didn't just say a prayer for the man lying half dead on the side of the road or politely respect his dignity by turning his head away to give him some privacy during his suffering. He didn't tell the beaten man that God willed his suffering, or it would create character, or it was for a purpose he better not interrupt. The Good Samaritan was moved to action. The way the Samaritan washed feet in that situation was by practically helping and caring for someone in need.

Sometimes it's not enough to just offer spiritual support. We need to wash feet in a practical way. Some of us are invited to do this as a life calling, like Mother Teresa, and others of us simply need to be open to God's promptings in situations as they arise.

Some ordinary ways I've been a recipient of footwashing in everyday life:

- A man gave me a pair of his shoes to wear after the earthquake because I ran out of the building with bare feet and there was rubble and broken glass everywhere.
- A friend brought over food when I was sick.
- My beautiful housemate left me cash and a little note to get some groceries when I had no money for food that week.
- One of my friends patiently listened to me weep on the phone multiple times when I was going through horrible heartbreak.
- While I was studying overseas a housemate helped purchase my travel ticket so I could spend Christmas with her family.

HOW OFTEN HAVE I WALKED PAST?

> "Then they also will answer, 'Lord, when did we see thee hungry or thirsty or a stranger or naked or sick or in prison, and did not minister to thee?' Then he will answer them, 'Truly, I say to you, as you did it not to one of the least of these, you did it not to me.'"
>
> Matthew 25:44–45

When I see a need, am I often moved to meet it? What are practical ways I can wash feet?

Love is more than an intangible concept, or a feeling, or an impulse. As missionary Heidi Baker says, "Love has to look like something."[1]

TWENTY-TWO

The Temperature of the Water

If you've been burned, you're more likely to be shy of hot water. When I was a kid, I accidentally fell onto a metal bar heater and burned my face. What made me more cautious in the future wasn't the memory of the heater burning me, but the discomfort of a numb face from the ice-cold water I had to keep on my skin for twenty minutes afterwards.

Just as Jesus washed us (His Bride) with the water of the Word, we are called to use the same water as we minister to others. But the temperature of the water we use matters.[1]

The Rare Times I've Preached the Gospel Outright

I can only remember two clear times in my life when I have preached the full gospel message to someone outright. Once was with a woman practicing witchcraft, and the other conversation was on a beach in Asia with a young Hindu man who was asking me questions about the meaning of life. In both conversations, they *wanted* to hear the full gospel story.

Both conversations ended with me clarifying that they couldn't have "Jesus and." The woman needed to know she couldn't give her life to Jesus *and* continue with witchcraft. The Hindu man needed to know he couldn't just add Jesus as another god amongst many. If you're doing a

"Jesus and" spiritual journey right now, I urge you to put your full trust in Jesus and let go of the other things. Tarot cards don't have a plan for your life. Jesus would never leave your life to the flip of a card. Crystals and rocks don't know your name. Freemasonry won't set you free. Karma isn't compatible with the gospel because Jesus took punishment for what He didn't do and gave us forgiveness we hadn't earned.

Most of the time I feel like the most effective approach and what someone's heart needs isn't a bold, in-your-face conversation about the gospel, but a gentle approach. So many people are wounded and have misconceptions about Jesus, God, religion, and Christianity. With this in mind, the temperature of the water with which we wash feet matters.

Scalding Hot Water

Scalding hot water is how people get burned by Christians. Hot water looks like all passion and no consideration for feelings—whether someone is ready to hear what you have to say, or how what you're saying might impact them. It's taken a long time for me to realize that just because something is truth doesn't mean I'm representing Jesus well when I say it. Even the Enemy can quote Scripture (Jesus' temptation in the wilderness, Matthew 4:1–11). Plenty of people have been wildly hurt, misled, and controlled by Scripture taken out of context.

God gives us instructions on how we can communicate truth in a way that can be received in 1 Corinthians 13. It's the classic passage often read at weddings:

> "If I speak in the tongues of men and of angels, but have not love, I am a noisy gong or a clanging cymbal. . . .
>
> "Love is patient and kind; love is not jealous or boastful; it is not arrogant or rude. Love does not insist on its own way; it is not irritable or resentful; believes all things, hopes all things, endures all things."
>
> 1 Corinthians 13:1, 4–7

Truth and love cannot be separated. Both are aspects of God's nature. He is Truth: "I am the way, and the truth, and the life" (John 14:6). But He is also love: "God is love" (1 John 4:8). To be like Him, we have to be both of those things. The apostle John wrote,

> "Beloved, let us love one another; for love is of God, and he who loves is born of God and knows God. He who does not love does not know God; for God is love. . . . If any one says, 'I love God,' and hates his brother, he is a liar; for he who does not love his brother whom he has seen, cannot love God whom he has not seen."
>
> 1 John 4:7–8, 20

The way we act shows the fruit of our hearts and lives. When we treat others in a hurtful way, we are revealing a gap in our experience of the God of love, who has only been loving toward us, no matter how we have behaved toward Him.

We need truth balanced with love as we wash the feet of people.

Have I been burned by water that's "too hot"? Have I burned anyone else?

Stone-Cold Water

Stone-cold water may feel to the recipient like you're treating them as a project or you don't care about them at all. There is a disconnect between the actions and the heart behind them. A person might feel like an item on a checklist—and it hurts to feel like someone is interacting with you out of obligation. Imagine having someone reluctantly washing your feet or doing it out of a sense of duty.

While burning someone with hot water might look like overemphasizing truth and leaving love behind, sometimes we can do the opposite and give a half-hearted wash with cold water. Our own fear of rejection can lead to tepid water that has no impact, or worse, mistakenly creates damaging affirmation of behavior or beliefs.

There are times when God calls us to be brave and speak truth rather than avoid it, even to preserve peace. Jesus values peace . . . but not a false peace at the price of truth. That's simply avoiding conflict until it inevitably reappears at a later time.

Do I avoid conflict? Would I prioritize avoiding conflict over truth?

Warm but Not Lukewarm

As imitators of Jesus, we're aiming for anything but lukewarm—warm enough to wash off grime, cool enough it won't burn. A temperature found somewhere in the middle, between overly passionate and maintaining peace.

Different people will receive temperatures differently. There isn't one temperature that will work for everyone. If someone has been burned before, they will need cooler water than someone who's used to room-temperature water. Someone who's only ever experienced icy cold water needs warmer water.

The only way we can know which temperature to use as we engage with them in conversation is through asking the Holy Spirit. This is why I've only ever come in with scalding hot water a rare few times in my conversations about God with people. I felt prompted to from the Lord, and I was received with openness and curiosity by the people themselves. It might seem obvious, but perhaps we can trust that people might tell us themselves which temperature they are ready to have their feet washed at.

TWENTY-THREE

Separating Identity from Behavior

Youth Prisons

"How are you feeling?"

"Great!" I squeaked out, a little too high to be totally convincing. Was I great? I wasn't sure. I hadn't been to a prison before, so I didn't exactly know what to expect. I was enroute to a youth prison in Australia with a team of chaplain volunteers. The fear didn't set in until I was going through security inside the prison—it was intense.

The warden walked us into a bare concrete room and shut the door. We were immediately swarmed by teenage boys who were honestly bigger than my father. The smallest was eleven, and the main chaplain immediately took him aside to check in on him, pray with him, and ask after his family. I knew she was worried about him.

I whipped out a pack of playing cards and asked with more confidence than I felt, "Uno, anyone?" I strategically sat with my back against a wall, and the boys sprawled out in a half circle around me. They joked and jostled amongst each other and tried to tell me what they were in prison for, and I tried not to listen. Things escalated quickly as one of the young men stacked Draw Two cards onto another player's hand, and I rolled out of the way as they scuffled on the floor, game forgotten.

Separating Identity from Behavior

The second youth prison visit in another state in Australia felt completely different. The boys were the same, but security was much more casual, and after some lunch and basketball hoops, we gathered a group of young men together in the chapel. We worshiped together, prayed, and unpacked some Scripture. Looking around, I had a moment of realization—yes, these teenage boys had made poor, perhaps even horrific choices. But their crimes didn't determine their identity any more than mine did. They were still sons, loved by the Lord. Sons who had probably made bad decisions, but still beloved sons Jesus took pride in. He looked at them and saw future leaders, business owners, fathers, husbands, engineers, creatives, sports players. He saw young men He'd created to be uniquely strong, soft, easygoing, intense, intelligent, musical, sensitive.

How does God see me? Who did He make me to be?

Identity as a Child of God

> "So through God you are no longer a slave but a son, and if a son then an heir."
>
> Galatians 4:7

Attempts to destroy identity are not new tactics from the Enemy. They began in the garden with Adam and Eve, continued through Jesus' time on earth, and still persist today. The serpent in the Garden of Eden planted seeds of doubt about God's identity as well as our own. "Did God really say that?" "You aren't good enough as you are, you're missing something" (cf. Genesis 3:1–6). It was insecurity about identity that contributed to Adam and Eve's separation from God.

The beginning of Jesus' public ministry shows similar tactics of the Enemy. Right after Jesus was baptized and a voice from heaven declared, "This is my beloved Son, with whom I am well pleased" (Matthew 3:17), Jesus followed the Spirit into the wilderness and the Enemy attacked His identity: "If you are the Son of God . . ." (Matthew 4:1–11). The Enemy constantly pressures Jesus to question and prove His identity.

The Woman Caught in Adultery

We have long made the mistake of turning our actions into our identity. It's a strategy of the Enemy to keep us locked into our shame. For example, the woman caught in adultery in John 8. The Pharisees wanted to stone her (as the Law required) as an adulterer. The Enemy called her "Adulterer." But Jesus saw her differently. He didn't condemn her but instead was able to separate her sin from her inherent identity and value.

When it comes to identity, there's a difference between the voice of the Enemy and the voice of God. God says, "I forgive you, you are not your sin, and I believe in you to choose differently next time." The Enemy says, "You will never change because you *are* your sin."

What things in our own lives has the Enemy managed to convince us are our permanent identity? Lying? Mismanaging finances? Cheating? The labels that become our identity don't even have to be sin related. We could have made "Pastor" our identity, or "Mother" or "Introvert." Perhaps a label we've put too much of our identity into is around our sexuality. Sexuality, while a part of you, is not your identity. Your identity is that you are a loved Son or Daughter.

What are the areas of my life that the Enemy has tried to convince me are my permanent identity?

Who else have I labeled by their actions?

One of the main reasons we disqualify anyone from sitting down on the footwashing seat is that we believe their behavior is their identity. When we're able to separate someone's actions from their inherent worth as Jesus does, we label them not based on their past, but based on

God's good future for them. The Lord looks at those young men I met in prison, and He doesn't call them "Thief" or "Gang Member." He calls them "Son." When we're also able to separate someone's behavior from their identity, no one will seem too scandalous to sit on the footwashing seat with Jesus.

TWENTY-FOUR

Go Where the People Are

Bar Ministry

Everyone in my ministry school served in a weekly outreach activation, and I cried when I found out I'd been assigned to bar ministry. I was ready to lead worship in the healing rooms or work with at-risk kids. But drunk people in bars? That was not my thing. I didn't like drunk people, or loud music, or sleazy men, or sticky floors, or drugs, or bars. So bar ministry was *way* outside of my comfort zone.

The first year was rough.

If I cried when I was assigned to it in my first year, I choked when I opened the email and had been assigned to the same ministry again in my second year. I wasn't sad; I was angry. "I specifically wrote on my activation application *not* to put me into bar ministry again!" I fumed.

At five to midnight on Good Friday, we got the usual roundup cue from our team leader, and in the middle of the karaoke bar with lights flashing red and green and blue, I froze and yelled at him, "I think I'm going to do something stupid!"

"What?" He struggled to hear me over the music, and confusion covered his face.

"Never mind!" I flapped my hands and tried to hide the panic on my face. "I'll meet you outside!" I nodded at him, and he gave me a confused smile and walked off to gather the rest of the team.

I took a quick breath but didn't give myself time to pause and think. It was like one of those moments where you are about to throw yourself off the end of the diving board, or off the edge of a waterfall into the water below, and if you think about what you're about to do you'll chicken yourself out of it. So I just switched my brain off and let my legs walk me briskly over to the closest table to do what I was convinced God asked me to.

"I'm so sorry to interrupt, but I just have to tell you—do you know that Jesus loves you?" Two men in their forties stared at me like I was crazy. I repeated this at every single table in the bar, yelling over the top of the music. One burly young man said, "Me? Jesus loves me? Still? Why?" Another big, middle-aged fellow told me he'd never heard that before, and *my* eyes just about popped out of *my* head. "No one has ever said that to you? No one? Well, it's true!" He thanked me and gave me a hug.

I didn't have time to linger in conversations as I dashed between tables, quickly telling everyone about the love of God, who had died for them on the first Good Friday. I kept looking over my shoulder, knowing I was racing the bouncer, who would quickly realize what I was doing and kick me out of the bar. I bolted outside and joined our group in the parking lot, adrenaline pumping through my veins. I felt like my eyes were so bright and alert and wide I still could have seen in the dark if the streetlamps went out.

It was a night that changed something for me. Bar ministry went from a hassle, an obligation to respectfully fulfill, into a choice. Two men had never heard that Jesus loved them before—and they thanked me for telling them. They were hungry to hear it. And I had the privilege of sharing it with them.

Not Everyone Has Heard the Gospel

The Enemy would love us to believe the lie that everyone has already heard the gospel, has heard that Jesus loves them. It makes sharing about Jesus with people feel like overstepping a boundary; as if people have heard and rejected God already, and you're pushing past a decision someone's already settled on.

But that's a lie.

One from the pit of hell, in fact. Such a simple strategy from the Enemy—stop the Christians from spreading the good news in the first place.

Do I think that everyone has heard the gospel? Do I hesitate to share the gospel because I presume people have already made their decision about Christianity?

The reality is this—not everyone has heard the gospel. Even in nations the gospel has already reached. The two men in the bar that night who had never heard that Jesus loved them were in California, USA. Not a jungle in unexplored regions.

According to the research gathered by the Joshua Project, approximately two billion people on the planet have yet to hear about Jesus.[1] That's around one in four people who haven't had an opportunity to adequately hear the gospel in a way that enables them to make an informed, free-will decision.

Go to Where the People Are

Jesus went into "bars" to wash feet. He didn't invite people to meet Him at the "holy" temple filled with "holy" people. He entered into the real, messy, come-as-you-are lives of people. For example, He went to the home of Zacchaeus, a chief tax collector who received him "joyfully" (Luke 19:2–10). One of my favorite parts of that passage is that Jesus had people murmuring about His actions, disturbing religious culture and flipping tables.

> "And when they saw it they all murmured, 'He has gone in to be the guest of a man who is a sinner.'"
>
> Luke 19:7

I HOPE PEOPLE HAVE A REASON TO MURMUR AFTER SEEING THE WAY I LIVE OUT THE GOSPEL

Jesus is Emmanuel—"God with us"—God coming to the people as they are instead of the people having to come to Him all cleaned up.

Jesus called himself a "friend of tax collectors and sinners" (Matthew 11:19; Luke 7:34), but I wonder how many of us would be comfortable calling ourselves a "friend of fallen pastors and abortionists" or "a friend of same-sex couples and scammers."

Would I be comfortable being called a friend of sinners?

As Jesus said himself when others questioned His choices to spend time with people living in public sin, He came for the lost. And you won't find the majority of the lost in churches. We all need our feet washed by Jesus, but some people haven't even heard yet that there's a stool available to sit down on.

> "For, 'everyone who calls upon the name of the Lord will be saved.' But how are men to call upon him in whom they have not believed? And <u>how are they to believe in him of whom they have never heard?</u> And how are they to hear <u>without a preacher?</u>"
>
> Romans 10:13–14

↳ THAT'S US!

TWENTY-FIVE

Reach for the Towel, Not Rocks

We're Stoning People

Some of us are stoning people in the process of learning what Jesus thinks and what He would do. The Pharisees were a prime example as they brought the woman caught in adultery to Jesus.

> "Early in the morning he came again to the temple; all the people came to him, and he sat down and taught them. The scribes and the Pharisees brought a woman who had been caught in adultery, and placing in the midst they said to him, 'Teacher, this woman has been caught in the act of adultery. Now in the law Moses commanded us to stone such. What do you say about her?'"
>
> John 8:2–5

TURNED A PERSON INTO A LESSON

The Pharisees and Scribes didn't bring the woman caught in adultery to Jesus because they cared about her, or even cared about sin or justice. She was a victim of their desire to test Jesus and discover who He was—and in their case, to try to condemn *Him*.

> "They said this to test him, so that they might have some charge to bring against him."
>
> John 8:6 NRSVA

Some of us are making people He loves collateral damage as we try to figure out who Jesus is and how to bring His truth and heart to situations. I've stoned too many people as I've learned more about His truth but left His heart behind.

I'll never forget finding out that multiple friends of mine had abortions when they were younger. My heart grieved, and I wondered how often my passionate words on the topic of abortion had unknowingly hurt my friends. It was a horrible reality check about whether I'd been unintentionally conveying condemnation or inflicting more pain through my communication around the prolife cause. I'd been accidentally "stoning" parents who had chosen abortion and left no room for compassion or healing. I was too quick to throw stones instead of picking up a towel to wash, tend, mend.

Am I quicker to pick up stones or pick up a towel to wash feet?

Part of me wonders whether one of the reasons Jesus protected the woman was because He knew firsthand what it was like to nearly be stoned to death. Within the same Bible chapter (John 8), and possibly even on the same day, a mob tried to stone Jesus too:

> "Jesus said to them, 'Truly, truly, I say to you, before Abraham was, I am.' So they took up stones to throw at him; but Jesus hid himself, and went out of the temple."
>
> John 8:58–59

The Only One Qualified to Throw Rocks, Didn't

> "Jesus bent down and wrote with his finger on the ground. And as they continued to ask him, he stood up and said to them, 'Let him who is without sin among you be the first to throw a stone at her.' And once more he bent down and <u>wrote with his finger on the ground</u>."
>
> John 8:6–8

[Handwritten note: WHAT WAS HE WRITING?? SINS OF THE SCRIBES + PHARISEES?]

We don't know what Jesus wrote in the dust. One theory is that He wrote out the sins of the Pharisees, demonstrating that they also had sin in their own lives. Whatever He wrote, and whether the Pharisees could see it or not, Jesus' words convicted each of them to eventually walk away.

I'm not worthy to condemn anyone else. Jesus would have plenty to write about me in the dust if He wrote out failings. As the sinless, perfect one, Jesus was the only one qualified to throw a stone, and He didn't.

I'm not worthy to condemn anyone, but I *am* able to pick up a towel and help bring restoration.

TWENTY-SIX

Wash and Be Washed

Jesus in the Australian Outback

It was the screams at night that kept me awake. We were in Wadeye (Port Keats) in the Northern Territory of Australia for around a week, and I didn't sleep. Every night while I lay on the floor on sofa cushions, locked inside a house—which was locked inside something similar to a gigantic cage, which was surrounded by a gigantic fence with a locked gate—it was the noises at night that kept me awake. Women screaming, men fighting, and what sounded remarkably similar to gunshots . . . or was gunshots.

My work on a youth missionary team meant I had the privilege of being invited into Indigenous communities across Australia. We held faith encounter nights for anyone who wanted to come, and the highlight was always the retreat we would have out in the bush, where we would set up camp with local Indigenous families in remote areas for days on end. We prepared meals together (I was on dishes duty . . . one person kept watch for crocodiles while the other washed pots in the ocean), sang worship songs, swam in a crocodile-free waterhole, prayed together, learned about their beautiful culture, hunted for food (I stuck to hunting seafood), and gave simple talks on who God was. The weeks we spent in a variety of particularly remote Australian bush and island locations with Aboriginal communities are some of my most memorable, for both the best and the toughest reasons.

The hostility of Indigenous toward non-Indigenous Australians stems from a long history of colonial oppression, including the forcible removal of Aboriginal and Torres Strait Islander children (the Stolen Generation) from their families and communities by government authorities to be assimilated into white Australian society. Additionally, Indigenous Australians faced forced labor, police brutality, and systemic racism. As I stayed and heard their stories, I wasn't surprised there was so much intergenerational trauma and ongoing tension. The way people can, have, and still do treat each other based on the color of skin is unthinkable. We have abused the Lord in the living temple of others when they haven't looked like us.

Wash and Be Washed

I'm no expert on social justice, cultural relations, or healing racism, but I have to believe that I know someone who does have an answer: God.

When I think of the trauma of racism, the footwashing analogy comes to mind as a way we can disrupt cycles and pursue healing.

Asking to wash someone's feet when you've both been hurt by each other can hold multiple meanings. It can represent an apology and repentance, and it can also represent forgiving someone as you pour water on their feet.

It's unlikely you will have the opportunity to literally wash the feet of many people throughout your life, so this footwashing will likely be more symbolic and practical. It can take the form of an apology for the way you've treated someone, or it may look like inviting someone to a table they've previously been excluded from. It may look like implementing justice where there's been injustice, restoring things that have been lost. (Double portion restoration is biblical.)

> "Instead of your shame you shall have a double portion, *IT'S BIBLICAL!*
> instead of dishonor you shall rejoice in your lot;
> therefore in your land you shall possess a double portion;
> yours shall be everlasting joy."
>
> Isaiah 61:7

THE ENEMY LOSES WHEN HE STEALS FROM ME

After Zaccheus the tax collector encountered Jesus, he didn't just restore what he had stolen from people as he collected taxes, but he was convicted to restore four times what he had unjustly taken (Luke 19:8).

Do I need to restore anything to anyone? Have I been a part of injustice or exploitation?

Often more challenging than washing feet is letting someone wash your own feet, whether it's literal or symbolic. There's a tension in us that resists letting someone "wash our feet" because it means letting go of the right to be offended by their behavior toward us. Or maybe it's pride? Once you forgive someone, you have agreed to give them a blank slate and release them from your judgment. You can't continue stacking up their offenses against you. Holding on to offense against someone leaves you with a sense of control over them. They owe you, and they are the enemy and reason for your unhealed pain.

How do I respond when a person who's hurt me gives me an apology? Am I able to accept it?

What would I do if someone wanted to make peace with me, offer a just solution, and move forward together?

I know that racism is a massive conversation. There are so many contributing factors and situations. But I know that racism breaks His heart, and He has restoration on His mind. And I wonder whether our hesitation about letting other people wash our feet is a part of why cycles of brokenness continue. I'm convinced that footwashing holds a key to the solution for racism.

TWENTY-SEVEN

Forgiving Your Parents

The way you've experienced your parents will often influence your view of God. If you had a parent you felt pressure to perform perfectly for, you might think you have to be perfect or win awards to earn God's approval. If you had to compete for your parents' attention, you might feel as though you need to earn God's attention by doing really good things or being a "better Christian" than other people. Maybe you think He's only proud of you if you're in a leadership position. If you had a parent who was frequently angry, you might expect God to be quick to punish you, keeping a chart of all your good and bad behavior with a reward and punishment system. If you had an absent father, it could be more difficult for you to connect with God the Father compared to other figures in the Trinity.

I don't know if there's anyone on the planet who hasn't been disappointed in some way by their parents. I believe part of the maturing process looks like growing in compassion and gaining perspective on our parents and the ways they've hurt us. We begin to understand that they're also people with stories and wounds of their own.

Jesus died for them, for their shortcomings and weaknesses and pain, just as much as He did for ours.

Giants in My Promised Land

I love the analogy that the giants we kill in our lifetime are ones our children won't have to face in their promised land. It stems from the Israelites' refusal to enter the promised land for fear of the giants. As a result, instead of entering their promise, they wandered in the wilderness for forty years until the fearful generation had died, and then their children were the ones who entered the promised land and confronted the giants their parents hadn't.

The next generation will have to face the giants we don't deal with.

When you look at your parents, you might feel as though there's a hundred giants running around that you have to face because they didn't. But (hopefully) you also see some major Goliaths that they overcame so you didn't have to. Those giants could represent things like cycles of poverty, abuse, moral failure, death, fear, sexual immorality, addiction, failed marriages. If you look at your parents and what they've faced in their lifetime, there's a high chance you'll see graves of giants behind them too. Maybe they overcame domestic violence or adultery. Maybe the fact that they can say "I love you" to you is a breakthrough when they were raised to repress emotion.

What is my promised land?

What are the giants in my promised land?

What are the giants my parents overcame?

I have made it my mission to take out as many giants as I can, but I know my children will still grow up and look at their promised land and see giants I let live, missed, or even fed.

Father to the Fatherless

While some have grown up with a parent who hurt them through their actions or words, others grew up with a parent who was absent altogether. There is a pain there to be processed and healed in a particular way with the Lord.

The good news is that none of us are truly an orphan—we have a Father who is intentional about having relationship with us.

> "Father of the fatherless and protector of widows
> is God in his holy habitation."
>
> Psalm 68:5

> "For you did not receive the spirit of slavery to fall back into fear, but you have received the spirit of sonship. When we cry, 'Abba! Father!' it is the Spirit himself bearing witness with our spirit that we are children of God, and if children, then heirs, heirs of God and fellow heirs with Christ."
>
> Romans 8:15–17

I HAVE A GOOD FATHER

The Perfect Parent

God is the only perfect parent for us. He is slow to anger. He doesn't impulsively punish us. He doesn't have wounds which show through in the way He treats us. He doesn't manipulate, doesn't let fear dictate His actions, doesn't speak harshly or discourage our dreams.

> "You, therefore, must be perfect, as your heavenly Father is perfect."
>
> Matthew 5:48

God the Father will never

- Leave you
- Disappoint you
- Ignore you
- Manipulate you
- Physically hurt you
- Abandon you
- Compare you to anyone else
- Expect you to perform
- Criticize you

- Humiliate you
- Punish you
- Use you
- Abuse you
- Break His word

God is the kind of Father who will always

- Cover you
- Want relationship with you
- Be proud of you
- Know your name
- Choose you
- Know who you are made to be
- Believe in you
- Speak positively over you
- Correct you gently, not out of anger but calmly, with love
- Control His temper
- Have time for you
- Search for you in a crowd
- Fight for you
- Die for you
- Wash your feet

Whether your experience of your parents has been generally positive or extremely painful, every single one of us needs a relationship with God the Father. He is the only perfect parent, and our heart is hungry for His affirmation, His attention, His affection, His protection, His generosity, His provision, His comfort, His fathering. There is a longing inside all of us which only God the Father can fill.

Some of us need to see our parents on the footwashing stool, having their feet washed by Jesus. We need to release them from our judgment and blame. One day, there's a chance we will need to have Jesus wash our feet as a parent too, and I think you might hear Him say

"I know you're doing your best. I'm really proud of you for all those giants you've slayed. You have what it takes. I forgive you for your downfalls. I believe in you still, and even though you might feel like you've made a mess, there's no way you can mess up your children so much that I can't fix them. I love you. Let me wash your feet."

TWENTY-EIGHT

Run Toward Prodigals

If Jesus calls people from all walks of life, that includes celebrities. We don't seem to have any problem with the idea of the middle class coming home, but the outcasts? The famous? Now that challenges us.

We All Need God

It's fascinating (and worrying) to observe how a significant portion of Christians react toward the public announcement of the conversion of a celebrity. There's a whole range of reactions: suspicion, doubt, celebration, immediate acceptance, wariness, even a sense of jadedness. I think many Christians feel disappointed by the way many Christian celebrities have historically (mis)represented Jesus, and it colors their response with a hesitation to extend support too quickly. Along with celebration, there is a strong "older brother" attitude that emerges. When the Prodigal Son returned home, the older brother refused to celebrate, still upset with his younger brother's previous behavior and the celebration for the younger brother despite his terrible misdeeds (Luke 15:25–32).

> *How do I usually respond when someone announces they've become a Christian? With skepticism or welcome?*

The Mistrust of Saul/Paul's Conversion

Watching public figures be met with suspicion instead of open arms by Christians reminds me of Acts 9. The disciples were so suspicious of Saul/Paul's life-changing encounter with Jesus that most of them immediately rejected him from the Christian community. Only one man, Barnabas, was willing to take a risk and put faith in the Lord's ability to radically change a life and bring Saul into the community.

[handwritten note: I WANT TO BE A 'BARNABAS']

> "And when he had come to Jerusalem he attempted to join the disciples; and they were all afraid of him, for they did not believe that he was a disciple. But Barnabas took him, and brought him to the apostles, and declared to them how on the road he had seen the Lord, who spoke to him, and how at Damascus he had preached boldly in the name of Jesus."
>
> Acts 9:26–27

Reading through Paul's conversion makes me wonder how many times celebrities have a genuine encounter with God but Christians reject them because they don't look like a Christian from the moment they come out of the baptismal water. We look for history, for evidence, for transformation, for fruit, but they only became a Christian and had Jesus wash their feet . . . hours ago.

How radically different did your life look twelve minutes, twelve days, even twelve months after you encountered God? It's through spending time with Jesus that we look more and more like Him. I was baptized at fourteen, but it took seven years of being surrounded by believers for my life to START to externally transform in a significant way as the Lord taught me about my identity, and Christian friends and leaders poured into me. I remember being surprised when I received an intentional invitation to join a Christian leadership program for a select number of young adults. I didn't look like a Christian leader yet, but someone believed in me. Someone ran toward me while I was still "on the road."

When someone tells me they've encountered God and they're now a believer, I want to instantly run toward them like the father bolted down the road to his Prodigal Son, not let suspicion rob someone of discipleship and community. Maybe the reason we see some celebrities (and others!) get baptized and then fall away from the faith is because we say, "They don't look like a Christian yet, so I don't want to welcome them into the family," and they're denied community with the very people who are called to form new disciples—Christians. Us.

"Go therefore and make disciples of all nations, baptizing them in the name of the Father and of the Son and of the Holy Spirit, teaching them to observe all that I have commanded you."

Matthew 28:19–20

It's true; perhaps some celebrity conversions aren't as genuine or long-lasting as we'd hope, but only Jesus can truly know someone's heart. And I'm convinced that the way to ensure genuine and long-lasting conversions is through discipleship and Christian community. Jesus didn't say, "Go therefore and get someone to say the sinner's prayer and leave them to figure out the rest alone." He said, "Go therefore and make *disciples*."

I don't want to be the older brother in the Prodigal Son story, who resents the celebration for the younger son's return. I want to be the first to run forward, yell "Welcome home!" and wash the dirt off their feet from where they've walked.

TWENTY-NINE

Feeding Celebrities to Lions

Lunch with Johnny Depp

In my early twenties I wandered through an airport in Australia, mind on the lunch I'd just bought at a kiosk. I sat down at the first table I spotted with room near my boarding gate. Mid-munch I absentmindedly glanced up to see who was across the table from me and noticed distinctive tattoos on the man's hands. I kept eating, focused on texting a friend, but the tattoos stayed at the back of my mind. Eventually they fought their way to the surface, and my eyes widened as I realized I recognized them as the tattoo designs actor Johnny Depp had on his hands. Startled, I looked at the man again and realized I was indeed sitting at a table with Johnny Depp. He kept a hat pulled low over his face and sunglasses on, and I wondered whether to start a conversation with him. The only thing that came to mind was, "Do you know Jesus?" and I was convinced that if I opened my mouth, that was all I'd be capable of saying. As I sat and wrestled with whether to say anything to him, security arrived and escorted him onto the plane.

Depp vs. Heard

Years later, the public legal battle between Johnny Depp and his ex-wife, actress Amber Heard, unfolded. I don't usually pay attention to celebrity news, but after my unusual encounter with him years earlier, the drama between these two prominent celebrities caught my interest. The public court battle became a popular point of discussion between friends as we debated who we thought was innocent or guilty, the evidence, and frankly, the scandal. The social media algorithm pushed clips from the court hearings to the top of my newsfeed to scroll through. Thanks to the accessibility of the internet, I was able to livestream the court proceedings, and it was grim. I switched it off with a heavy heart, confronted by the fact that while I had judged through thirty-second social media reels, and a jury judged after the court hearing, only God judged by truly knowing the hearts of the people involved.

Regardless of who was victim and who was perpetrator, they both needed Jesus equally—just as desperately as the rest of us.

> ONLY GOD TRULY KNOWS A HEART — MOTIVES, WOUNDS, SOMEONE'S STORY.

> "For the LORD sees not as man sees; man looks on the outward appearance, but the LORD looks on the heart."
>
> 1 Samuel 16:7

Listening to the details of the court case, I was shocked to realize that the day I sat opposite Johnny in that Australian airport was apparently during the heart of the pain of his turbulent marriage. My heart ached as I remembered the one question that burned on my heart to ask him. I wondered what God might have done if a young woman who accidentally sat at a table with him had had the courage to respond quickly to His prompting. I know God is not mad or disappointed in me for hesitating, and who knows how that conversation may have unfolded. But recognizing that I missed an opportunity to partner with the Holy Spirit to reach someone in the middle of deep pain motivates me now to respond quickly to God when I feel Him ask me to say or do something. I don't want anyone to miss out on an encounter with God because I'm afraid of looking silly.

When you move past the fact that these were two very famous celebrities locked in a public battle, you start to see that they were two people in a public battle as a result of brokenness.

Celebrities have children. They want desperately to be loved just as much as you and I. They have gifts to offer the world. And wouldn't it be just so beautiful if, as humans, and ESPECIALLY as Christians, when people lay open all their brokenness for the world to see, we cover them instead of exploiting them in their vulnerability?

I have absolutely been guilty of turning someone's mess into my entertainment.

Today's Roman Arena

Once upon a time, the horror of Christians being fed to lions in an arena was entertainment for the secular world. I know this is different, but I hope that when Christians see anyone, whether a believer or nonbeliever, in pain, we don't pick up popcorn and settle in for the show. On a spiritual and social level, this is today's way of throwing people to the lions and watching for entertainment. I believe we are meant to be people who turn away, who provide a place of safety for the exploited, who step in to help. We are meant to pick up a towel and wash feet, not pick up popcorn and cheer as people go through the worst time of their life.

The reality is that we aren't only guilty of sending celebrities to the arena. We enjoy the delightful horror of gossip about our neighbors, reading articles with the morbid details of someone's marriage ending, and watching reality TV shows where seeing a relationship implode is what we relax to. We have numbed ourselves to the pain of those around us and turned that pain into our own entertainment. We can do better.

Am I guilty of turning someone's pain into my entertainment?

THIRTY

Protecting People

People Getting Their Feet Washed Are Vulnerable

When I visited Bethel Church for the first time, there was an altar call for people struggling with repetitive sin in their lives. It was an invitation for anyone who wanted freedom to run to the front, respond to God, and receive prayer. I felt like my heart was beating out of my chest. I desperately wanted to run forward, but I was afraid of being judged. Finally, as I watched many other people race to the front responding to God, my desire for freedom overrode my shame, and I hurried forward too. The front of the sanctuary was packed with people responding, and the second I reached the back of the crowd with my gaze fixed on the ground, hands touched my shoulders as strangers prayed simple prayers for freedom and restoration with me. There was no judgment, just a sense of being covered and met by love from the church. From Jesus, really. That night was a catalyst for my freedom.

I've looked back on that moment as a wonderful example of the church—Christians—doing what Jesus did. Meeting sinners with love. Not focusing on their failings but partnering with them to see freedom over their lives. It was a response of rushing to cover someone while they are vulnerable and feel dirty, like the father of the Prodigal Son running to meet him on the road home.

When someone is exposed, it is our mandate as Christians to cover them, not exploit or judge them. This is a part of how we wash feet. When someone brings their dirty feet to Jesus, sitting down and saying to Him, "Okay, Lord, I'm humiliated but I'm here, please wash my feet," that is when we have the opportunity to cover them while they are vulnerable and afraid of being rejected.

Jesus Protected the Woman at the Well

Needing to be met in the middle of feeling so utterly exposed reminded me of someone Jesus covered well during His earthly ministry. Remember the woman at the well?

Jesus met a woman at Jacob's well in Samaria. He broke cultural norms by speaking with a woman, let alone a Samaritan woman (there was tension between Jews and Samaritans, and Jesus was a Jew), and on top of that, she was probably a social outcast (public sinner) because she was fetching water at the hottest time of day while no one else was.

> "Jesus said to her, 'Go, call your husband, and come here.' The woman answered him, 'I have no husband.' Jesus said to her, 'You are right in saying, "I have no husband"; for you have had five husbands, and he whom you now have is not your husband; this you said truly.' The woman said to him, 'Sir, I perceive that you are a prophet.'"
>
> John 4:16–19

Jesus knew this woman and her sins, but here's what He didn't do: single her out in a crowd and call out sinful details of her life to prove He was God. It would have been an effective way of revealing to a large group of people His supernatural identity, but instead Jesus waited to meet her while she was alone in a private moment, so no one else would hear. Jesus didn't expose her to more of the same rejection and judgment she had already been living with.

Through their encounter, Jesus was revealed as God, the woman was met with kindness and confronted on her sin, and a whole city received the good news about the Messiah. And all of this was still achieved while protecting the woman who was the key to all of it unfolding.

> "So the woman left her water jar, and went away into the city, and said to the people, 'Come, see a man who told me all that I ever did. Can this be the Christ?' They went out of the city and were coming to him. . . .
>
> "Many Samaritans from that city believed in him because of the woman's testimony, 'He told me all that I ever did.' So when the Samaritans came to him, they asked him to stay with them; and he stayed there two days. And many more believed because of his word."
>
> John 4:28–30, 39–41

ONE ENCOUNTER CAN SAVE AN ENTIRE CITY

The woman chose to make her history and her testimony public knowledge. Jesus didn't decide that for her. He still met her in the middle of her mess—right in the middle of it—but He didn't expose her to punish her, make her change her behavior, or glorify himself. She was the one who told people of what Jesus had known about her life. Then it was her encounter with Him that led to the salvation of a large portion of a city. One person's encounter with Jesus can save a city.

We Must Cover Well

As Christians, it is our responsibility to cover people well. Not *cover up* sin but create a safe environment for people to admit to God they have dirt on their feet. It can look like keeping what people share with you private. It can look like being the person who breaks a chain of gossip about someone when it reaches you. It can look like keeping prayer requests or private conversations to yourself. In a church setting, covering can look like protecting someone's dignity when they are encountering God in an overpowering way, or coming quickly to cover when someone responds to an altar call. We don't focus on someone's sin; we remind them of their true identity. We pray with people for freedom, forgiveness, healing.

Do I create safety for people to bring their dirty feet to God?

It's vulnerable to acknowledge that we have dirty feet. It is really important when we invite people to the footwashing stool that we cover them too. Washing feet is an avenue of pastoral care.

We shouldn't want only to flip tables (call out injustice/sin)—we should be just as ready to wash feet.

THIRTY-ONE

The People Missing from Our Pews

Witchcraft in the Back Pew

"Tell her I'm glad she's here," the Lord whispered as a young woman passed me in the communion line. "Uh, okay?" I said back. Church ended and I slid out of the wooden pew and walked toward the back of the church, where the girl sat alone. All I had to go on were the Lord's words, "Tell her I'm glad she's here." I took a breath and inwardly joked with the Lord, "You always give me just one random line! Hope you know what You're doing!" I laughed at myself a little as I slid onto the back pew next to her with fake confidence and said brightly, "Hey! How are you?" It was mid-slide onto the pew that I realized the Lord had absolutely set me up. The young woman was unloading several bags' worth of pots, rocks, and salts onto the pew, and I had to push what looked like a cauldron filled with water and a massive quartz crystal of some kind to the side to make room to sit. "Lord, are you kidding me right now . . . ?" I said to Him inwardly, but I didn't mind. He was after the "one," and she was currently casting spells in the back pew of my church.

I introduced myself and asked what she was doing. She was distracted but friendly as she explained that someone had cursed her, and she was trying to counteract the curse.

"Oh dear!" I said. "That does not sound good. Well, I'm so glad that you're here! I wanted to come and say hello and just tell you that God is so glad that you're here. Can I be honest with you, though?" I said with a smile, and she smiled back, giving me her full attention. "Sure!" I looked apologetically at her, but I meant every word as I said with the utmost conviction, "These rocks won't save you. Making a curse won't break the curse, it's only going to make it worse. The only thing that can help you is Jesus. Have you heard of Him?"

For the next forty-five minutes, I told this precious young woman about Jesus Christ. She kept listening and I held her gaze as I finally asked, "Do you want to give your life to Jesus right now?"

"Let's ****ing do it!" she said with all the enthusiasm she had. And there, amidst her rocks and salts and potions she came in hoping would save her, she gave her life to the Savior of the world.

Just because she didn't walk into the church a Christian didn't mean she didn't belong inside a church. She wasn't a lost cause or a waste of time. She wasn't the enemy. She was exactly the Prodigal Son (Daughter) that God was standing on the road looking and longing for. Too often we have people missing from our pews because we expect them to look like Jesus before they've even met Him.

The Jesus Movement

Tens of thousands of people were baptized in Pirate's Cove in Newport Beach, California, during the Jesus Movement of the late 1960s and 1970s. The movement saw many young people, including hippies, turn to Christianity and be welcomed into church instead of rejected. Chuck Smith, the pastor of Calvary Chapel in Costa Mesa, California, played a key role by opening his church doors to these young people despite initial resistance from members of his congregation.

I wonder who the hippies are today that I'd be uncomfortable with if they tried to walk into my church? Perhaps today's equivalent could be the LGBTQ+ community? New Age? People "deconstructing" their faith? Gen Z?

A key Bible verse often associated with the Jesus Movement was Matthew 11:28:

THOSE WHO MOST NEED HIM

"Come to me, all who labor and are heavy laden, and I will give you rest."

PROMISE

Matthew 11:28

Don't Gatekeep the Footwashing Seat

There are people missing from pews because we expect them to look like Jesus before they've spent any time with Him. We gatekeep the church doors and make it uncomfortable for anyone to enter without feeling judgment, and we ask people who mess up to leave to keep other people comfortable.

Who might be missing from my church community?

How do I react to people coming to church who don't fit in or act in a way I like?

I wonder how many of today's hippies would fill our pews or line up for footwashing if we let them through the front doors instead of gatekeeping the footwashing seat.

THESE ARE THE PEOPLE MISSING FROM OUR PEWS BECAUSE WE ASK THEM TO LOOK LIKE JESUS BEFORE THEY'VE SPENT ANY TIME WITH HIM.

THIRTY-TWO

Canceling Cancel Culture

I suspect for many of us, it might feel more instinctual to put this chapter on sexuality under the next section of the book labeled Enemies, rather than within the section labeled Friends. But that's exactly what I want to talk about.

I refuse to let the Enemy make us enemies.

True and False Unconditional Love

There is an ongoing goal of the Enemy to divide humanity, and one of the main tactics is through the belief that unless we all unconditionally accept and support each other's choices, we cannot be connected. This is a twisted version of true unconditional love, which says "No matter your choices, I won't withdraw my love from you." Love becomes a weapon when used as a manipulative tool. Love is no longer love when it can be sold, won, bought, earned, or lost.

I believe that we see this clearly through what we currently identify as "cancel culture." It is a collective social behavior that intentionally excludes, ostracizes, and publicly isolates a person as a result of their words, behavior, beliefs, or choices. There have been times when the public withdrawal of support from someone or something has been a form of taking a stand against injustice, but I am concerned by the way our society has taken on a culture of canceling and alienating anyone who doesn't think, act, and believe the same things we do. It is an unhealthy belief system that declares, "If you don't support my choices, you don't love or respect me."

Do I push people away who don't support my choices or beliefs?

This is a dangerous mindset when it comes to any kind of relationship. It turns us into people wanting to surround ourselves with clones of ourselves. It's hard to build trust or move past surface level with anyone who holds a constant threat over you that if you disagree or challenge them, they'll end your connection. Fear and control are the biggest motivators in relationships like this and leave no room for dialogue, making mistakes, forgiving, growing, and learning.

I particularly dislike the way I see the influence of cancel culture over the topics of sexuality and gender (and I'm not insinuating it's one-sided.) There is a huge pressure to "agree with me or be canceled" from both perspectives, at a personal as well as professional level.

In the midst of all the well-intended-yet-unhealthy attempts to maintain relationship and offer respect to those we find ourselves disagreeing with on significant issues, this phrase has been on my heart:

I refuse to let the Enemy make us enemies.

Because you know who wants us divided? The Enemy.
You know who wants us to feel like we're enemies? The Enemy.
You know who wants us to think there's only one answer when we disagree, and it's permanently broken relationship? The Enemy.
You know who wants us to believe pushing people away is the only option when they don't look like us? The Enemy.

But you know who wants us to live at peace with our neighbors? The Prince of Peace.

You know who wants us to maintain relationship with people even when they're walking in sin? The Friend of sinners.

You know who wants us to forgive quickly? The Redeemer of the world.

You know who wants us to be surrounded by people different from us? The Good Shepherd.

You know who wants us to treat each other with honor? The King of kings.

I know sexuality is a particularly sensitive topic for many people. And I don't think that anyone is under the impression that collectively as a society, or a church, we've nailed a healthy approach for how to navigate conversations and relationships around this. There's still room here for Jesus to teach us how to act like "kings."

Step One: An Apology

As I mentioned earlier, I was part of a team who ministered in all kinds of bars across the city every Friday night. One particular week I struck up a friendly conversation with a man sitting near me in a gay bar. Once he discovered I was a Christian, it didn't take long for him to share that his parents were pastors of a big church in town, and he'd felt really hurt by them and the way they'd treated him with regard to his sexuality. I apologized on behalf of Christians who had hurt him, and we hugged and he thanked me for the apology.

It was the pattern I saw over and over as I ministered to

people who were a part of the LGBTQ+ community—the first step in their journey with God was actually to receive an apology from a Christian after Jesus had been misrepresented to them with water that was way "too hot." These men and women felt burned by Christians because of the way they'd been treated—with judgment, condemnation, exclusion, humiliation. Apologizing on behalf of Christians didn't mean I was affirming their choices or saying that God would support their gender/sexuality beliefs—it was simply saying sorry for where people had been hurt.

Am I able to offer an apology or show love to people without following up with justification or conditions?

Maybe washing feet in this season looks like letting people who've been told there's no space for them on the footwashing stool know that Jesus is there, kneeling and waiting for them still if they ever want to sit down. Maybe it's letting someone know that Jesus calls them Son or Daughter, and that's what defines them. Maybe it's apologizing, being a "minister of reconciliation."

> "Therefore, if any one is in Christ, he is a new creation; the old has passed away, behold, the new has come. All this is from God, who through Christ reconciled us to himself and gave us the ministry of reconciliation; that is, God was in Christ reconciling the world to himself, not counting their trespasses against them, and entrusting to us the message of reconciliation."
>
> 2 Corinthians 5:17–19

Don't let the Enemy make you enemies with anyone.

Have I let the Enemy make me believe someone is my enemy?

Enemies

If you are human, someone has wounded you. And in all likelihood, the very last place you want to see your enemy is on the footwashing stool. Or maybe your enemy is someone who represents everything you stand against. How can the same seat be open for them *and* you?

This section, Enemies, may feel like the most challenging, but it could also have the most significant, real impact on your life. Perhaps the very thing you need is found in this last section. Be brave. Jesus washed the feet of His enemies too.

THIRTY-THREE

He Washed Judas's Feet Too

It all comes down to this: If Jesus washed Judas's feet, Jesus would wash anyone's feet.

When we look at Jesus washing Judas's feet during the Last Supper, it destroys all our protestations and hesitations about whose feet Jesus would wash.

> "And during supper, when the devil had (already) put it into the heart of Judas Iscariot, Simon's son, to betray him, Jesus, knowing that the Father had given all things into his hands, and that he had come from God and was going to God, rose from supper, laid aside his garments, and girded himself with a towel. Then he poured water into a basin, and began to wash the disciples' feet, and to wipe them with the towel with which he was girded. . . .
>
> "When Jesus had thus spoken, he was troubled in spirit, and testified, 'Truly, truly, I say to you, one of you will betray me.' The disciples looked at one another, uncertain of whom he spoke. One of his disciples, whom Jesus loved, was lying close to the breast of Jesus; so Simon Peter beckoned to him and said, 'Tell us who it is of whom he speaks.' So lying thus, close to the breast of Jesus, he said to him, 'Lord, who is it?' Jesus

[margin note: THIS WAS HARD FOR JESUS]

answered, 'It is he to whom I shall give this morsel when I have dipped it.' So when he had dipped the morsel, he gave it to Judas, the son of Simon Iscariot."

John 13:2–5, 21–26

> HE KNEW, AND HE STILL WASHED.

The key here is that Jesus knew Judas had and would betray Him, and He still chose to wash his feet anyway.

"Betrayal—I know that one."

On their seventh wedding anniversary, a young wife knelt and washed the feet of her husband. She spoke over him about his purity and goodness as she washed his feet, sharing promises that the Lord had given her for the ways she was going to love, serve, and choose him during their upcoming year of marriage.

Two weeks later, she was lying curled up on the floor of their bedroom in deep emotional pain after finding out that her husband had been unfaithful. While she lay there, she said to Jesus, "I'm so alone. I have no idea what to do. I don't know how to move forward from this. I know my husband has just had a big encounter with you, but I don't know how to see him any other way." She saw Jesus lie down on the floor opposite her, mirroring her curled-up position, as He said, "Betrayal—I know that one. I washed Judas's feet too."

When she had washed the feet of her husband two weeks earlier, she was unknowingly washing the feet of her betrayer and speaking over who he was becoming. And now, as she lay on the floor, face to face with Jesus, He reminded her of the things she had spoken over her husband, the promises she had given for their marriage as she washed his feet.

The next night she asked her husband if she could wash his feet again, this time knowing how he had betrayed her and still choosing to wash his feet. She felt Jesus' hands join hers, telling her, "You can do this. This is how we love," as she repeated all the same promises and declarations over her husband again.

Does this story offend me? Why?

This couple—my friends—has given me permission to share their story because I don't know how else to better illustrate what Jesus did for us when He washed feet. He washed the feet of the people He already knew would betray Him. Judas. Peter. Nearly all His friends. The next day they would be the ones to sell Him out, deny even knowing Him, abandon Him while He died naked in agony on a cross. Judas had already betrayed Him to the high priests as Jesus knelt and lovingly washed his feet. Jesus washed the feet of His unfaithful Bride, spoke identity, renewed covenant promises, made sure we knew we would always be loved and welcomed back by Him.

Witchcraft in the Pew: What Happened Next

Do you remember my friend involved in witchcraft, who gave her life to Jesus in the back of the church? I want to tell you the second part of her story.

I nearly missed her because she looked so different, but sure enough I saw the young woman who'd given her life to Jesus amidst her crystals and curses sitting in church again. I genuflected as the last note on the piano rang through the church and bolted for the back of the church, weaving through grandmas gathering their handbags and raincoats as I made a beeline for my new friend. "Hey!" I had raced through the church so fast I was borderline needing to catch my breath. "I'm so glad to see you! How are you? How are you and Jesus going?"

We chatted about her newfound love for Jesus and the radical way she'd encountered God and left witchcraft behind. She told me she now had a Bible and had just read the Gospels for the first time. "What's your favorite part?" I asked her, curious, and she answered me instantly with triple the intensity of our conversation to date.

"*Judas.* That guy!! When he betrayed Jesus I"—her eyes bugged and she was lost for words—"I literally jumped up and threw the book down! I couldn't believe it! If I was Jesus, I would have thrown fists!"

"And yet . . . Jesus loved him! Wild, huh!"

She wasn't done. "Yeah, but if I was there I woulda—like if Jesus was here I'd be like, 'Just say the word, Jesus, and I'll shank him for you!!'" (With extra cussing.)

My friend's reaction to discovering the story of Judas's betrayal of Jesus for the first time reminded me of how awful it really was. Sometimes when we hear something so many times, overfamiliarity can steal the true impact. What Judas did was horrendous—and Jesus, knowing that, knowing what was coming and who would betray Him, still chose to wash Judas's feet. He didn't exclude Judas, or create some distance, or quietly send him out to buy more food for the Passover while He washed the other eleven disciples' feet (as the disciples thought Jesus had when Judas left the dinner later on [John 13:29]). Jesus continued to offer relationship, lean in close to Judas, right until the very end.

Have I become so familiar with the story of Judas's betrayal that it has lost its impact on me?

Here are some things we can learn from Jesus washing Judas's feet:

1. Jesus washing Judas's feet was clearly not a symbol of affirming Judas's actions. Footwashing is not affirmative of behavior, beliefs, or choices.
2. Giving your life to Jesus is not a prerequisite for receiving footwashing, since Judas had already rejected relationship with Jesus.
3. Jesus did not reject anyone from the footwashing seat, no matter who they were or what they'd done. It is available for everyone.

THIRTY-FOUR

Honoring Our Enemies

It's how we treat Judas, not Jesus, that reveals the true state of our hearts.

How we treat the people we like, agree with, and who treat us well in return says absolutely nothing about our character or heart.

How we treat the people who hurt us, disappointed us, betrayed us . . . that says everything about whether we think being worthy of respect is dependent on good behavior.

> "He said also to the man who had invited him, 'When you give a dinner or a banquet, do not invite your friends or your brothers or your kinsmen or rich neighbors, lest they also invite you in return, and you be repaid. But when you give a feast, invite the poor, the maimed, the lame, the blind, and you will be blessed, because they cannot repay you. You will be repaid at the resurrection of the just.'"
>
> Luke 14:12–14

God's love isn't a prize to be earned or deserved. He doesn't treat us with respect because we've earned it. He doesn't show greater honor to the people who've not sinned for a longer amount of time. If God waited to treat us with respect until we'd earned it, we'd still be waiting. None of us deserve what He freely offers us.

Do I think people need to earn my respect? Did Jesus wait for me to earn His respect before He gave it to me?

How Jesus Treated Judas

Jesus taught us how to treat our enemies by the way He treated Judas. Jesus treated Judas so well that no one suspected Judas was the ultimate betrayer.

It's not as if Jesus wasn't aware of what Judas was planning. If Jesus had been in the dark about Judas's agreement to hand Him over, the way Jesus treated Judas would tell us nothing about how to treat our enemies. It's because Jesus was *already* aware of Judas's betrayal that the way He treated Judas tells us everything.

Jesus continued to offer relationship and restoration to Judas without holding back from him. If it were me, and I knew a friend of mine was planning on betraying me, the first thing I'd do would be create distance and put up walls between us as a way of protecting myself. I would cut that person out of my life ASAP. I certainly wouldn't choose to invite them to spend the last night of my life with me. But what did Jesus do? He continued to offer relationship to Judas with so much of the same openness that no one had any reason to wonder whether Jesus was treating Judas differently.

Jesus Healed His Enemies

What was Jesus' last miracle He performed before His death? It was healing His enemy's wound. In the Garden of Gethsemane during Jesus' arrest, Simon Peter cut off the right ear of Malchus, the high priest Caiaphas's slave, but Jesus defended and healed the man (Luke 22:50–51; John 18:10). Jesus, the true High Priest, healed a wound He hadn't caused and took the punishment for crimes He had not committed.

Jesus didn't treat His enemies the way they deserved.

Serving Your Enemies

Culturally, the old covenant teaching of the Law of Moses that the Israelites lived by was to repay any grievances or offenses "in kind" as a form of justice, e.g., "an eye for an eye" (Leviticus 24:19–20). But Jesus gave us a new commandment in the new covenant:

Enemies

"You have heard that it was said, 'An eye for an eye and a tooth for a tooth.' But I say to you, Do not resist one who is evil. But if any one strikes you on the right cheek, turn to him the other also; and if any one would sue you and take your coat, let him have your cloak as well; and if any one forces you to go one mile, go with him two miles."

NEW COVENANT *OLD COVENANT*

Matthew 5:38–41

His radical servant king posture and example He left us is not to treat well only those who treat us well, but to treat everyone with love, kindness, and honor. Specifically, even those who are our enemies.

Jesus continues,

"You have heard that it was said, 'You shall love your neighbor and hate your enemy.' But I say to you, Love your enemies and pray for those who persecute you, so that you may be sons of your Father who is in heaven; for he makes his sun rise on the evil and on the good, and sends rain on the just and on the unjust."

Matthew 5:43–45

Do I treat everyone with the same respect, dignity, honor, willingness to serve?

Why am I more eager to serve an important leader than an unknown stranger on the street?

It is easy to serve and honor those we like. But how are we serving those we don't like, who don't treat us well? This is what makes Jesus a radical servant king—His willingness to serve everyone the same. His friends and His enemies.

THIRTY-FIVE

Politics

Believers Should Look Different

What if Christians set the standard for the world for how to treat people you disagree with, even those in leadership? It's possible.

This isn't just about election season, and it's not just about politics. It's about the way we interact and treat any leader or person in our life who holds a different opinion than we do—and election season is a prime example of the opportunity to do this.

I hope election season and politics are a chance for believers to shine differently than the world. In a culture that's mocking, dividing, even turning to violence over politics, I hope Christians demonstrate something different is possible. Peace. Honor. Hope. Treating people with dignity. And a deep trust that no matter who is in leadership, God is still on the throne.

Does my behavior change during election season or when the topic of politics arises? Am I proud of the way I speak and behave? What's behind the way I act?

> "Let no evil talk come out of your mouths, but only such as is good for edifying, as fits the occasion, that it may impart grace to those who hear."
>
> Ephesians 4:29

I don't know why, but during election season, we seem to think we get a free pass to treat people as horribly and disrespectfully as we want. We say demeaning things about candidates, and we attack and scorn those who have different political opinions than us. Plenty of us say things Jesus would count as truth, but we sound way more like the voice of the Enemy than the voice of God in the process of saying it.

Look to Daniel and Joseph

When we look to Scripture for how we should treat our leaders, we see figures like Daniel and Joseph serving leaders with honor. They didn't compromise on following God, but even when those in authority were behaving badly or were their enemies, Daniel and Joseph continued to be an example of treating people with honor and respect.

Honoring someone doesn't mean agreeing with them or supporting their opinions or stances. This is true, even of *our* leaders! But honor means we treat everyone with respect and with the dignity God gave them, no matter what they do.

We are called to a higher standard, and not just during political debates or elections. Imagine what could change if we walked through every election season, every tense discussion, every online platform with this level of honor. Christians could (and should) revolutionize the political sphere and the world with radical honor.

It is a mistake to try to judge anyone's heart or relationship with the Lord. Yes, the fruit of someone's life tells a story of what's inside their heart, but it's a dangerous game to try to judge a leader's relationship with the Lord. We don't know whether any leaders would, or truly have, sat down on a footwashing stool with Jesus. But here's what we do know: The footwashing stool is open for anyone. Including leaders. To say there is someone whose feet

Jesus wouldn't wash is to say there's someone He didn't die for, so we need to be very careful when we make statements about someone's salvation status—in any direction.

If we have concerns over our leaders, let's pray for them to be wildly encountered by God. Pray for wisdom for them.

We can be different.

> "You are the light of the world. A city set on a hill cannot be hid. Nor do men light a lamp and put it under a bushel, but on a stand, and it gives light to all in the house. Let your light so shine before men, that they may see your good works and give glory to your Father who is in heaven."
>
> Matthew 5:14–16

LOOK LIKE GOD.
REPRESENT HIM WELL.

THIRTY-SIX

A Heart for Both Sides

It was my third attempt at visiting the Middle East. The first time my tickets to Egypt and Israel were canceled because of war. The second time my flights to Jordan and Kuwait were canceled nine days before departure due to the global pandemic. So my third attempt still felt dubious right up until I made it through customs and stepped foot onto a Middle Eastern street. I was in disbelief, and in heaven.

It's true what God says about himself—He is a great Redeemer. He takes the double-portion promise seriously. Within the space of sixteen months, I had returned to the Middle East not once, not twice, but three times, and visited more countries and regions than I ever expected to.

What in my life do I need God to redeem? Am I expectant for a double portion?

Shattered in the Middle East

The first time I spent time in the Middle East, my heart got absolutely shattered for the underground church and persecuted Christians. I was rocked to meet people, hear their stories, and realize that it was not just a few bold or unprotected ones who were persecuted for following Jesus, but pretty much everyone.

I reeled as I sat across a table from a man who had been tortured. Tears poured from my eyes as I prayed for a distressed young mother wondering how to protect her toddler. I barely knew how to take in the man who'd never heard a worship song. We were the first Christians he'd seen in two years. These were the moments that made me wonder what on earth I had to offer people who had survived so much. My faith felt untested—I had been through some pain and survived a natural disaster, but I hadn't ever faced a cost for following Jesus like this.

In the book of Acts, Peter responds to a man begging for alms at the temple gate by telling him he doesn't have anything tangible to give, but he can give an encounter with Jesus. It's not a perfect analogy, but in a way, that is how I felt in this moment too—I only had one thing to give, and it was Jesus.

> "But Peter said, 'I have no silver and gold, but I give you what I have; in the name of Jesus Christ of Nazareth, walk.'"
>
> Acts 3:6

I returned from that first experience in the Middle East feeling cracked wide open. I cried every day for a week as I sat in my safe mega church seat, surrounded by six hundred ministry school students who had no idea what was really happening to our Christian family on the other side of the world. I had been well and truly wrecked, and not in an entirely good way. All I knew was that my heart burned strongly for the persecuted church.

What does my heart burn and break for? Could it be a clue about my calling?

While I was still in the Middle East the first time, I received an email letting me know I'd been selected to return to the Middle East again five months later, and my heart honestly sank. I wasn't sure I'd be ready to return to the Middle East again so soon. But five months later, with a new team, I was boarding the plane for two new countries in the Middle East. I genuinely felt ready to go.

I Need a Heart for Both Sides

It wasn't until we were walking through the streets in the Middle East again that I realized there was something churning around in my heart. "I don't want to minister to Muslims after meeting persecuted Christians on my last trip," I blurted out to my leader. It was an admission that surprised both of us. I genuinely didn't know I had that sitting in my heart. My heart was well and truly broken for persecuted Christians. "Perhaps the Lord needs to break your heart for Muslims too," he suggested. I doubted it.

A group of Muslim school girls spotted us tourists from a mile away and excitedly asked to take a group photograph with us. As we chatted with them, my heart softened a little.

I continued walking and as I spotted a pair of young women, I felt the familiar stir of the Holy Spirit in my heart. "I love them," He whispered. I pulled out my phone and opened Google translate and shared messages from the Lord, blessings, prayers with them. They loved it and wrote sweet messages back to me, thanking me.

As the call to prayer went up over the city, I stood and quietly prayed. "God, my heart still hurts over the persecution of my Christian brothers and sisters, often because of this religion." *I know*, He said. *What do you think they most need?* I paused and realized, "It's You. What they most need is You." It was a revelation that rocked me, and in that moment my heart broke for "the other side" too.

The burden I carried, and why I kept going to the Middle East, was because people needed Jesus. Persecuted Christians desperately need the Prince of Peace. And the persecutors desperately need the Prince of Peace. I wasn't there to offer Jesus only to one side—but both. It was a true moment of realization for me, of seeing Jesus washing the feet of a persecuted Christian

as well as a Muslim. Up until that point I hadn't found it within me to draw Jesus washing the feet of a Muslim, but the image finally made sense to me as I had a revelation of Jesus' heart for the Muslim people. Of how desperate He was to have them answer His invitation to wash their feet and transform their lives too.

> "The Lord is not slow about his promise as some count slowness, but is forbearing toward you, not wishing that any should perish, but that all should reach repentance."
>
> 2 Peter 3:9

The chair that I meet Jesus on—the same footwashing stool—is also theirs. My chair is their chair.

Can I see "both sides" on the seat?

THIRTY-SEVEN

Prostitutes at the Dining Table

Trafficked

"Look away." God the Father's voice breathed in my head. "Look away or you'll give yourself away and never be let inside." It took all my willpower to break off the incredibly intense staring contest I was engaged in with the madam standing at the doorway to the establishment in the Middle East, physically change my face into a pleasant smile, and step past her into the room. I hadn't expected to get caught in the doorway by this woman, her normally dark eyes glinting an electric blue thanks to contact lenses. It's one of the few times I felt like I wasn't looking at a woman, but staring down Satan instead. And I wasn't about to look away first. If it hadn't been for the Father's voice in my head warning me to break eye contact so I could follow my small team into the room, I suspected I would have ended up waiting outside or pulling my entire team out.

Inside the "café" trafficked women of all ages sat and attended to men smoking shisha. My stomach plummeted as I saw a young girl standing in a doorway in a black abaya and hijab, who I estimated to be only fifteen or sixteen. I felt sick. We sat and sipped black coffee as slowly as we could to give us more of a chance to connect with the women working. We struck up some translated conversation with one of the women serving us, and much to my joy, a baby was plopped down in my lap. I cuddled the little girl and spoke God's protection and blessings over her. I told her she was going to have a different future than what was laid out in front of her.

Her mother was a young woman—unwed with two babies, generally unacceptable in Muslim culture—and the young woman's mother herself was the madam I'd had a stare-down with at the door. I hoped I was wrong in connecting dots that led me to think the mother was exploiting her own daughter.

We wrote on the receipt in Arabic that God loved her and hurried out, praying that the seed we planted would take root and grow into something that might change the future for that baby girl being raised in a brothel after generations of abuse.

> *Do I believe that God can radically interrupt unhealthy cycles at any time and change generations to come? Are there any generational cycles in my family I need the Lord to break?*

Pimp

"In your teams, spend some time praying and asking the Lord for clues about who He wants you to minister to tonight. It could be clothing, an image, hair color, anything." The teams huddled throughout the room and asked the Lord for insight before we even reached the bars—after all, He knew who He had on His heart that night to reach, even if we hadn't physically arrived there yet.

"All I saw was the overwhelming color blue," Austin from our team told me afterward during our debrief at In-N-Out. "I didn't know he was a pimp. I just knew the Lord had told me to look for someone in blue all over and there he was—head to toe in blue." Austin's bar ministry team had walked in the doors of the bar, and he instantly noticed the man dressed in a blue suit, complete with a blue waistcoat, blue top hat, and blue cane. So he walked up, struck up a conversation that opened with

"Cool cane!", proceeded to tell the man that God loved him, and offered to pray for him. It wasn't until afterward when the rest of his team told him the man was a pimp that Austin realized who he had been ministering to. He'd just treated him the same as anyone else God had highlighted to him throughout the year.

If God prompted you to, would you minister to someone even if you knew "who they were"?

Here's the Thing

Here's the thing.

Everyone loves the stories of Jesus dining with prostitutes, until a prostitute walks into church.

Everyone loves the stories of Jesus inviting tax collectors to join His ministry until a leader with a history of financial fraud is invited to the table.

Everyone loves the strange act of Mary emptying her perfume onto the feet of Jesus until someone starts to worship in a way they're uncomfortable with.

Everyone loves Jesus talking with the woman at the well until the girl living with her boyfriend shows up at youth group.

Everyone loves Jesus ripping apart the Pharisees and Scribes until someone breaks an unspoken church culture rule.

Playboy Playmate

Recently a Playboy Playmate liked one of my images on social media. As I scrolled down her page wondering who she was, my surprise turned to sadness at the exploitation of her body. I sat at my dining table, stumped that a person who would display their naked body inside a sex magazine would be interested in pictures of Jesus. I doubled back and checked which picture she had liked—it was one of Jesus kissing the forehead of a girl, and the text overlay read, "Not mad at you, madly in love with you."

Ultimately, I believe that Jesus died for everyone. I believe that for each of these people I've told the stories of—the madam, the trafficked women,

the unwed mother, the baby girl in the brothel, the pimp, the Playboy Playmate—Jesus is just as interested in reaching them as anyone else. They are the "woman at the well" people to whom Jesus would say, "I know your story; I'm God, and I've come for you." I don't ever want to be the one to say, "You're not who He came for."

Have my words or behavior ever communicated, "You're not who He came for"?

> "But God shows his love for us in that while we were yet sinners Christ died for us."
>
> Romans 5:8

PAY ATTENTION TO THE TIMING

We don't flinch when we read about Jesus dining with tax collectors, prostitutes, and sinners in passages like Mark 2:15–17, but we sure do flinch when people living an overtly sinful lifestyle today want to step foot into the presence of the Lord. But we're doing church wrong if we think the people most in need of God don't belong in His house.

Would Jesus wash the feet of a prostitute?
Would Jesus wash the feet of a trafficked woman?
Would Jesus wash the feet of a madam?
Would Jesus wash the feet of a pimp?

Maybe one day I won't grit my teeth as hard at the thought of someone who has abused others being welcome on the same seat, at the same table with the Lord as the victims, but it doesn't matter what I think or how I feel. It matters what Jesus does. He is after every single one of us.

THIRTY-EIGHT

Today's Tax Collectors

It's no secret that for the Jewish people, and in the context of Scripture, tax collectors were a big deal in a bad way. I find that reading about tax collectors has a low impact on me, because today I honestly really appreciate my tax accountant who helps keep my business afloat! But 2,000-odd years ago, being a tax collector represented something very different.

Historically, Jewish tax collectors were men who had betrayed their people by working for the enemy to assist with the exploitation of their friends, family, and community. They worked for Rome and for their own gain. They are classified as "robbers" in rabbinical writings.[1]

Jesus Chose a Tax Collector

If Jesus was trying to gain positive influence over the Jewish people, spending time with those who had betrayed them—let alone adding a tax collector to His disciples—was not the way to do it. Matthew would have been despised by Jews and viewed as a robber and traitor.

And yet . . . Jesus still chose him. And by doing so, He reached more than just one man. This is the call of Matthew from the Gospel of Matthew:

> "As Jesus passed on from there, he saw a man called Matthew sitting at the tax office; and he said to him, 'Follow me.' And he rose and followed him.

Enemies

"And as he sat at table in the house, behold, <u>many tax</u>
<u>collectors and sinners came and sat down with Jesus</u> and his
disciples. And when the Pharisees saw this, they said to his
disciples, 'Why does your teacher eat with tax collectors and
sinners?' But when he heard it, he said, 'Those who are well
have no need of a physician, but those who are sick. Go and
learn what this means, "I desire mercy, and not sacrifice." For I
came not to call the righteous, but sinners.'"

Matthew 9:9–13

HE SAT AT A TABLE WITH PEOPLE (BEFORE) THEY FOLLOWED HIM

Here's what I notice in this passage. First, Jesus invites Matthew, a tax collector, to follow Him. Jesus reaches one person. Then, Jesus sat down, and "many" tax collectors and sinners came and sat down with Jesus and His disciples. Reaching one meant reaching many.

We can surmise that Jesus didn't share a meal with many *former* tax collectors and sinners. No—he sat down with one former tax collector (Matthew—former as of perhaps a few hours), His disciples, and many *current* tax collectors and sinners.

There is a popular argument in today's Christian culture that Jesus' spending time with sinners was justified because afterward they converted and followed Him. They sat down one way and got up different. But this passage makes it clear that this isn't necessarily true. Sometimes it is (e.g., the calling of Matthew), but what about Matthew's friends? It doesn't say anything about them getting up from the table different from how they sat down.

I see footwashing this way. The open seat is not conditional upon your guaranteed acceptance of Jesus as your Lord and Savior. You are welcome to sit down, and it is up to you whether you get up the same way or different. It is your choice whether you let the encounter with Jesus change your life.

Does this challenge the way I view footwashing? Or view Jesus?

It is almost automatic in Christian culture to see those who are living lives opposite to the Gospel and say, "We better stay away from them." But Jesus did the opposite—He ran toward the tax collectors. I want to look at the lost and think, *They're exactly who I should run toward.*

Failed Church Leaders

It's easy enough to talk about tax collectors, but what if we actually replace them with a modern-day equivalent? What if we talked about extending grace and making room at the table for today's fallen church leaders? This topic instantly becomes uncomfortable.

Many of us have been disappointed and perhaps even personally wounded by a church leader who abused their authority and badly misrepresented Jesus. Perhaps it was through moral failure, or mismanaging finances, or spiritual manipulation. Perhaps it was an exploitation of volunteers or abuse of vulnerable people.

> *Have I been hurt by a church leader? How did I respond to it? Have I walked away from church because of the actions of a church leader? Is this an area I need to invite Jesus into?*

I'm not suggesting we overlook justice. I'm definitely not making a statement about whether Christian leaders who have abused their position should be reinstated into ministry. But it's clear that Jesus wouldn't hesitate to go to the house, sit down at the table, or wash the feet of a tax collector or anyone else who has failed in their leadership. He is *always* wanting relationship with us, and I hope we keep that in mind when we interact with people, even disgraced church leaders.

But. There's something else I need to say too.

If you're someone who resonates with being disappointed from a distance or traumatized

up close by a modern day "tax collector" who abused their authority and exploited people, please don't give up on Jesus when He's the very thing you need. Don't walk away from Jesus because of the actions of people. Jesus didn't hurt you; Jesus didn't manipulate you; Jesus didn't abuse you; Jesus didn't betray you. Jesus cried while people did.

    Jesus can hold you while you cry.
    Jesus can comfort you.
    Jesus can heal you.
    Jesus can restore.
    Jesus can bring justice.
    Jesus can put you back together.

Jesus knows firsthand what it's like to be hurt, manipulated, abused, betrayed. Don't give up on Him when He's the very thing you need.

THIRTY-NINE

When They Don't Say Sorry

As we approach the end of this book, I'd like to address a pain point we all have in common—at some point, someone didn't say they were sorry, and it haunts us.

I want to talk about how to forgive and move on, even when we didn't receive the apology or experience the restoration we hoped for (yet).

Is there someone who I'm still waiting on an apology from?

Forgiveness Is Not the Same as Saying, "It's Okay."

Forgiveness is not saying, "It's okay."

Forgiveness is not necessarily saying, "I'm coming back."

But forgiveness IS saying, "I release you from my judgment, and I give up my right to revenge."

Forgiveness is not affirming someone's actions; it's giving yourself freedom to start the healing process and move forward.

Unforgiveness is one of the most socially acceptable sins of today. But just because it's normal or even encouraged (in an attempt to teach a lesson, or for self-protection), that doesn't mean it's healthy . . . or not a sin.

When They Don't Say Sorry

["Let all bitterness and wrath and anger and clamor and slander be put away from you, with all malice, and be kind to one another, tenderhearted, forgiving one another, as God in Christ forgave you."]

Ephesians 4:31–32

INSTRUCTION

God has given us an instruction over and over to forgive each other. And if He said it . . . I want to do it. I want to be more like Him, not less like Him.

Refusing to forgive someone is like standing in front of the footwashing seat and refusing to let them have access to it.

Take Back Your Power

The reality is, sometimes we won't receive the apology that naturally opens up the opportunity to forgive someone. But if we wait for an apology to be emotionally free and move on, we're leaving the key to our freedom in the hands of someone else. Many of us are familiar with the old proverb, "Unforgiveness is like drinking poison and expecting the other person to die."

We can't control what happens to us, but we can control how we respond to it. A victim mindset is believing we are powerless in the face of circumstances or people, making us ongoing victims to a person or event that continues to control and define us.

Some of us have been victims to very real circumstances and people; I'm not suggesting we pretend that isn't true. But I don't want the person or situation that hurt us to continue to have the strongest influence or final say over our lives.

INTIMIDATION TACTICS FROM A SCARED ENEMY

THIS IS WHO I'M MADE TO BE

"For God did not give us a spirit of timidity but a spirit of power and love and self-control."

2 Timothy 1:7

211

God did not make you to be a victim to the things that happen to you. He made you to be powerful. Forgiving someone is a step toward moving forward as a powerful person instead of remaining frozen in the past.

Steps to Forgiveness

1. **Acknowledge the extent of the pain someone has caused you.** Really be honest with how you've been impacted by their behavior. So often we run from feeling our emotions and push hurt under the metaphorical carpet. It's time to push back the rug or dig out the key to the box you've kept your hurt safely locked away in. It's a soft heart moment—opening yourself up to feel and experience the highs and lows, the victories and losses, God's heart for you and for others.

2. **Make an intentional choice to forgive the person.** Write down exactly what you're forgiving them for or say it out loud. It's important that we use clear language here to communicate what we're doing.
"I forgive _____ for *xyz*." You might not feel it, but you're making a powerful choice to release them from your right to judge them and to take revenge on them. It doesn't make what they've done okay. (This is why we always need to respond with "I forgive you" when someone apologizes to us, not "It's okay." It wasn't okay, but you are extending your forgiveness.) It's letting go of the anger and offense inside of your own heart toward someone and beginning the healing process.

3. **Bless them.** This may be the most countercultural part of the whole thing. As Christians, we're called not only to the challenge of forgiving people, but also to actually blessing our enemies. Spend time praying for the person who hurt you, asking God to forgive them and bless them. Pray that all God's good plans would be carried out in their life. Pray that they would have a radical encounter with God that would change their hearts. Pray that whichever wounds they have that led to their hurting you would be healed. Pray they have the courage to face the giants in their life.

And if God opens the door for you to bless them in a tangible way, be open to responding to Him in that too.

"You have heard that it was said, 'You shall love your neighbor and hate your enemy.' But I say to you, Love your enemies and pray for those who persecute you."

Matthew 5:43–44

> HIS WAY IS BETTER.
> HIS WAY IS HEALING.

You can carry out these steps in person if the appropriate opportunity presents itself, but you can also complete this forgiveness process in private. It's time to move on.

FORTY

Who You Need to See on the Seat

You already know who you need to see sitting on the seat. It's the reason you picked this book up in the first place. Maybe it was yourself. Maybe it was that family member you need to forgive, the friend who betrayed you, the boss who exploited you, the church leader who destroyed you.

The reason *The Footwashing Series* collected such an audience and following wasn't because the artwork was spectacular. It's not. I don't have an art qualification like my sister. I am not even particularly good at freehand drawing.

The reason the world watched with such anticipation is that everyone was waiting for the picture of *themselves*.

> The nurses waited for the picture of a nurse.
>
> The mothers waited for a picture of an exhausted mother.
>
> Those with anxiety waited for the images around mental health.
>
> The ones with church hurt are waiting for the image of broken church leaders and the people they've broken.

Maybe you've read this whole book cover to cover, hoping I would talk about your specific situation and how to navigate it. Waiting to see an image representing the person you most need to see on the seat. Needing to see yourself.

If the person you most need to see on the seat is you, this empty seat is for you.

If the person you most need to see on the seat is your enemy, this seat is for them too.

I know they hurt you. I know they disappointed you, crushed you, let you down. I know it feels like you might never recover from what they did to you. It feels more like you want to hurt them than see Jesus wash their feet. But what that person most needs to have a change of heart, a radical turnaround from their old ways, their "Saul-to-Paul" conversion . . . is Jesus.

> "I want my enemies to get saved."[1]
>
> David Hogan

Just as I realized what the people who persecute Christians need most is Jesus, what my own enemy needs most is an encounter with Jesus. Punishment might prevent someone from behaving a particular way again, but a transformational encounter with Jesus can stop a heart from ever *wanting* to behave that way again.

Who do I most need to place on the footwashing seat?

A Seat for You

This seat isn't just for the people we struggle with. It's also for you. I hope by now you've met a Jesus you *want* to encounter on the footwashing seat. I hope that if someone misrepresented Jesus to you, you've met the real Him and He's someone you want to know. I hope that if you were ever told Jesus didn't like you, didn't want you, or didn't love you, those fears have been erased.

I hope you have faced truths about Jesus and His love and what we're called to as Christians that have cut you to the core. I hope the words in this book cut deep, but I also hope the words here healed.

This is not a new Jesus. *The Footwashing Series* pictures might have contemporary people represented on the seat to help us see how footwashing still applies today, but this is not a diluted or new version of the gospel. It's just . . . gospel.

Everything that we've talked about in the pages of this book has been about the real Jesus and the way He wants to do relationship with us.

> He is the Father with arms open, looking for His Prodigal Son on the road.
> He is the Man at the well, waiting for the woman He knows.
> He is the Healer in a crowd, stopping for the one.
> He is the Friend of Sinners, sitting at a table with the broken.
> He is the Man in White, appearing in dreams.
> He is the Spotless Lamb, taking the punishment for our crimes.
> He is the perfect Bridegroom, staying faithful to the cheating bride.
> He is the all-deserving King, kneeling and washing our feet.

This is the God we can still encounter today. He hasn't changed. Do you know this God?

> The God with open arms, watching and waiting for you to come home.
> The God who waits for you, who truly knows you and loves you.
> The God who sees you in a crowd.
> The God with the power to heal you when nothing else can.
> The God who sits with you, even when no one else does.
> The God who finds a way to reach you, even when you aren't looking for Him.
> The God who paid the debt you owed.
> The God who stayed faithful to you, even when you wandered.
> The God who wants to wash your feet.

Will You Let Him In?

> "Behold, I stand at the door and knock; if any one hears my voice and opens the door, I will come in to him and eat with him, and he with me."
>
> Revelation 3:20

[Handwritten annotations: HE IS KNOCKING — HE WANTS ME; WILL I OPEN THE DOOR AND LET HIM IN?; THIS IS WHAT RELATIONSHIP WITH JESUS LOOKS LIKE]

If you feel like you know Him, but you want to be closer, pray this with me:

Jesus, cut me to the core with the gospel. I surrender every area of my life to You. King Jesus, here's the throne of my heart—I make way for You. Help me wash feet.

If you feel like you used to know Jesus, but it's been a while, and you want relationship with Him again, pray this with me:

Jesus, there's no one like You. Nothing else can satisfy. I'm sorry for wandering away from You and putting my trust in other things. You can have all my love, all my attention, all my affection. I want to go back to my first love with You. Please wash my feet.

And if you have never known Jesus in a personal way—maybe you've watched others be healed by the Healer, or sit at a table with Him, but you haven't met Him like this for yourself yet—today it's your turn to be seen in a crowd by Him. The footwashing seat is open to you if you want to sit down. If you're ready to have Jesus wash your feet and want a relationship with Him, pray this with me:

Jesus, I have dirt on my feet I need You to wash. Please forgive me for my sins and wash me clean. I want to know You, so please come into my life and teach me what it means to follow You. Fill me with the Holy Spirit, protect me with the blood of Jesus, encounter me with the love of the Father. I give my life to you. Amen.

It's still not about who's on the seat; it's about Who's washing the feet. Footwashing has only just begun.

Acknowledgments

I think it's normal to leave the biggest thank-you for last, but I hope my King is always the first thing spilling over my life. So my first words of gratitude go to this Jesus I've written about, who isn't just a concept but a Person. I hope I've made you proud and represented you well in this book.

And now, to the people who have championed, and at times carried me through, this process:

Mum, your roof has truly been my floor. There are many giants in graves because of you; I hope I slay half as many for my own kids one day.

My sisters, Melanie and Emma—you never once told me to give up on my calling and "get a real job." I think I would have cracked if I hadn't been believed in by you.

Dad, thank you for your unconditional support. Ministry wasn't what you expected for my career, but you're just as supportive as if I'd become an astronaut or Olympian. I'll never forget you and Nana, sitting sidestage in gumboots under a big top tent in a muddy New Zealand field while I preached to youth about footwashing.

Father Rob Galea, thank you for trusting me with a microphone to talk about footwashing on your 2024 concert tour throughout India. Footwashing came to life and so did I.

Kris Vallotton, I'm living in the legacy of sacrifices and faith-risks you took before I even knew Jesus existed. Thank you for inviting a student in your ministry college to talk about footwashing on your podcast. It opened the door for this book to exist at all.

Acknowledgments

Lisa Jackson, my literary agent—I'm really glad I didn't delete your email as spam after you heard my podcast interview with Kris and sent me an email that was surely too good to be true. You were convinced I had something to say. I never felt quite so believed-in as the moments you let us miss opportunities because you trusted my vision and God's plan for this book.

Jennifer Dukes Lee, my acquisitions editor—I knew Bethany House was the team for this book the second you opened our call with, "You don't have to prove yourself to us." You've been the voice of the Encourager throughout this process. Thank you for all the time zones we've navigated as you've chased me around the world during this process. I'm grateful to you and the Bethany House team for all the hard work poured into this book.

Father Ken Barker MGL, thank you for giving your time to theologically review this book and make sure I wasn't a heretic. I'm so grateful for your *yes* that led to the existence of the Missionaries of God's Love.

I've had a global village of people weeping with me in my losses and celebrating my victories. Heartfelt gratitude to my Bethel tribe in California, friends spread across Australia, my whānau in New Zealand, my Salt & Gold team, and the people in every corner of the world who make up the Salt & Gold online community. I've met the kindness of God through each of you, whether it was through prayer, letting me have a meltdown in your office, dropping off flowers to celebrate milestones, listening to me talk about this book *again*, yelling with joy in the Jeep as I received my first-ever offer on our way home from Napa, trusting me share a piece of your story in these pages, being patient when I dropped off the face of the planet to meet deadlines, or giving me prophetic words that feel twenty times bigger than what I see. I'm terrified in the best way of what God's done, and of what's still to come, and I'm thankful I'm not doing it alone.

Notes

CHAPTER 1 A KING IN A CROWD

1. "Passover," Jewish Virtual Library, accessed February 27, 2025, www.jewishvirtuallibrary.org/passover.

2. Alexander MacLaren, *Expositions of Holy Scripture* (London: Hodder & Stoughton, 1900), John 13, accessed February 27, 2025, www.studylight.org/commentaries/eng/mac/john-13.html.

CHAPTER 2 THE SERVANT KING

1. David Guzik, "John 13—Jesus, the Loving Servant," Enduring Word, accessed February 27, 2025, www.enduringword.com/bible-commentary/john-13.

CHAPTER 3 MORE RADICAL THAN WE THINK

1. Emil G. Hirsch, Wilhelm Nowack, Solomon Schechter, "Feet, Washing of," Jewish Encyclopedia, accessed February 27, 2025, www.jewishencyclopedia.com/articles/6051-feet-washing-of.

2. David Guzik, "Study Guide for John 13," Blue Letter Bible, accessed February 27, 2025, www.blueletterbible.org/comm/guzik_david/study-guide/john/john-13.cfm.

3. David Guzik, "Study Guide for John 13," Blue Letter Bible.

4. Hirsch, Nowack, and Schechter, "Feet, Washing of," Jewish Encyclopedia.

5. "Ketubot 61a:10," Sefaria, accessed February 27, 2025, www.sefaria.org/Ketubot.61a.10?lang=bi.

CHAPTER 4 TOO MUCH AND NOT ENOUGH

1. Marcus Dods, *The Expositor's Greek Testament: The Gospel of St. John, vol. 2* (Hodder and Stoughton, 1903).

2. Leon Morris, *The Gospel According to John* (Eerdmans, 1971).

CHAPTER 5 UNWORTHY

1. Adam Clarke, *The New Testament of Our Lord and Saviour Jesus Christ, vol. 2* (New York: Eaton & Mains, 1832).

Notes

CHAPTER 6 BARABBAS IS ME

1. Andrew Wilson, "The Story of Barabbas Is No Mere Prisoner Swap," *Christianity Today*, March 2021, www.christianitytoday.com/2021/03/andrew-wilson-barabbas-story-prisoner-swap.
2. Timothy J. Keller, "Mark 15:1–15, King's Cross: The Gospel of Mark, Part 2: The Journey to the Cross" (sermon, Redeemer Presbyterian Church, New York, March 11, 2007).
3. Timothy J. Keller, "Mark 15:1–15, King's Cross."

CHAPTER 12 IF YOU CAN'T GRAB HIS HANDS

1. Marvin R. Wilson, "Jewish Laws of Purity in Jesus' Day," Torah Class, accessed February 28, 2025, www.torahclass.com/archived-articles/1289-jewish-laws-of-purity-in-jesus-day-by-marvin-r-wilson and Joe M. Sprinkle, "The Rationale of the Laws of Clean and Unclean and Their Relationship with the Concept of Sacred Space," Alliance World Fellowship, May 28, 2018, accessed February 28, 2025, https://docslib.org/doc/6313755/the-rationale-of-the-laws-of-clean-and-unclean-in-the-old-testament-joe-m-sprinkle.

CHAPTER 18 TRUE LOVE AND FREE WILL

1. Kris Vallotton, *The Kris Vallotton Podcast*, "Cultural Catalysts with Jessica Bond—Transformational Art on Social Media," March 24, 2023, https://open.spotify.com/episode/0DeZDOhCAnOdRaUIgBYRkv.

CHAPTER 20 REPETITIVE FAILURE

1. Insurance Council of New Zealand, "Canterbury Earthquakes," accessed February 28, 2025, www.icnz.org.nz/industry/canterbury-earthquakes.

CHAPTER 21 LOVE LOOKS LIKE SOMETHING

1. Heidi Baker, "Love Must Look Like Something," YouTube video, 0:57, May 30, 2014, www.youtube.com/watch?v=YMnKzIXnSnQ.

CHAPTER 22 THE TEMPERATURE OF THE WATER

1. David Guzik, "John 13—Jesus, the Loving Servant," www.enduringword.com/bible-commentary/john-13.

CHAPTER 24 GO WHERE THE PEOPLE ARE

1. Joshua Project, "Has Everyone Heard?" accessed February 27, 2025, https://joshuaproject.net/resources/articles/has_everyone_heard.

CHAPTER 38 TODAY'S TAX COLLECTORS

1. "Tax Collector," Encyclopedia of the Bible, Bible Gateway, accessed February 28, 2025, www.biblegateway.com/resources/encyclopedia-of-the-bible/Tax-Collector.

CHAPTER 40 WHO YOU NEED TO SEE ON THE SEAT

1. David Hogan, in-person remarks, Bethel School of Supernatural Ministry, Redding, CA, December 2023.

Jessica Bond is the founder of Salt & Gold and is a communicator of the radical gospel through speaking, social media, and ministry. She is best known for creating the viral *Footwashing Series* artwork, illustrating Jesus washing the feet of people from all different walks of life.

With a background in youth ministry and missions, Jess has ministered in prisons, nightclubs, schools, underground churches, and crocodile-infested mangroves. After growing up in Aotearoa, New Zealand, and living in America, she is now based out of sunny Australia. Jessica is a graduate of Bethel School of Supernatural Ministry in California and calls the Catholic Church home.

Connect with Jessica:

SaltAndGold.com.au

@SaltAndGoldCollection

@TheFootwashingSeries

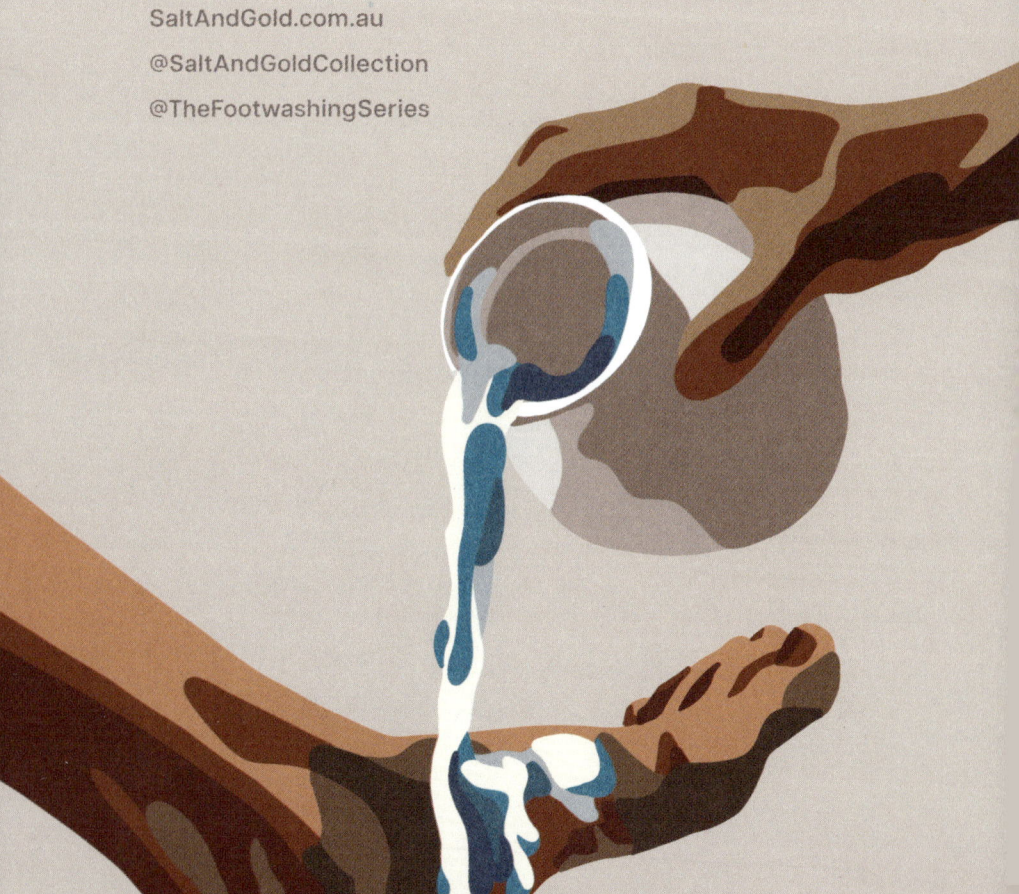